Rachel de Thame's
Top 100 Star Plants

Rachel de Thame's Top 100 Star Plants

Gardeners' World

For Gerard,
with love

contents

introduction

When it comes to gardening I am a great compiler of lists. I love to potter around a flower show, public garden or nursery with a notebook in hand listing all the plants I would like to grow. Narrowing these interminable sheets of paper into a selection of plants I can realistically give a home to, while bearing in mind the restrictions imposed by the size and growing conditions in my own garden is never easy. Like most insatiable enthusiasts, I covet many thousands of plants, while having room for only a fraction of them.

A visit to the garden centre or nursery can be fraught with temptation, so where do you start when faced with such a display of riches? Many excellent plant encyclopaedias offer page after page of mouth-watering suggestions, but beautiful photographs and reams of information can leave you feeling more confused than ever. Ideally you might prefer to get an informed recommendation from a fellow plant lover – and that is the purpose of this book.

Translating a wide range of plants into real life planting combinations in your garden can seem mystifying – I have simplified the process by narrowing the choices to a manageable selection. Each chapter includes some of my favourite 'cannot-do-without' plants – some to suit a typical garden situation, others to achieve a particular effect. Picking the final line-up was extremely painful, and the inevitable limitations of space necessitated my leaving out many worthy contenders, but those that made it did so entirely on merit.

Among the plants you will find old favourites, tried and tested over many years, and some that are less well known but deserve to be more widely grown. Many are key plants for me personally, evoking a memory of childhood or reminiscent of a time or place, while others have come to my attention more recently – during my travels for *Gardeners' World*, or while filming at a specialist nursery. I am frequently inspired by the knowledge and enthusiasm of both amateur and professional growers, and have rarely been disappointed by their recommendations for a new or unusual plant.

Ultimately you will form your own hit parade of favourite plants, but I guarantee that the following selection will provide a good basis from which to develop a garden. Putting the plants together is an art in itself, but many of those featured in any given chapter would work well together. In some instances I suggest possible partnerships and situations to get the best from that particular plant, and where appropriate I provide alternatives from the same genus, which offer a variation in colour, size or habit, to suit individual requirements.

So here – and with no apologies for individual taste – is my own, very personal selection of 100 beautiful plants that fulfil certain requirements or will be suited to specific uses. I have loved procrastinating about which to include, and enjoyed many long hours poring over the exquisite photographs. True plant lovers are always happy to share their experiences with others, and I hope this book will impart even a fraction of the enthusiasm I feel for these wonderful plants. Some are indisputably 'good doers', others are the objects of a recent infatuation. All are special to me – and I hope, after trying them for yourself, to you too.

plants for sunny, dry sites

Open, sunny areas are a blessing in any garden, as many of the loveliest plants require a position in full sun with a well-drained soil in order to thrive. South-facing beds and borders can be filled to overflowing with plants that capture the essence of summer with their vibrant colours in an endless choice of shades. A garden entirely devoid of direct sunshine may be subtle, calming and elegant, but it can also be lacking in sparkle and vitality.

Work with your sun-filled spot and create a garden in an appropriate style. Traditional herbaceous borders can be hard to beat, but do also consider modern-looking prairie and steppe planting schemes. Create a stunning backdrop for your plants by growing them through a layer of gravel or larger pebbles and allow annuals to self-seed and form unplanned combinations. Copy a Mediterranean courtyard adorned with terracotta pots, filling them with succulents and hardy palms for structure and annuals for colour.

Of course, sunny positions can be prone to water shortage, so if you want to avoid constant watering in hot weather – a high maintenance option that is far from environmentally friendly – you had better choose drought-tolerant plants. Selecting the right plants is the first step: giving them a helping hand is the next. If your soil is very thin and sandy, the rate of water loss will be increased significantly. Adding plenty of bulky organic matter will improve the soil structure and therefore moisture retention, while a thick layer of mulch, such as gravel, cocoa shell, or shredded bark, will minimise evaporation from the surface.

Heavier, clay soils also benefit from the addition of organic material, together with a generous quantity of horticultural grit to improve drainage. Drought-tolerant plants hate to have their roots sitting in cold, wet soil and many are lost in this way during the winter. By opening up the soil, you will give them a better chance of surviving to shine again the following summer.

Sun-lovers often have similar physical characteristics. Juicy, succulent leaves store precious moisture, releasing it gradually as required. Narrow leaves perform a similar function: their reduced surface area means that less moisture is lost through their pores. A waxy coating is another way to combat loss of water, as is a silvery sheen created by the reflection of light on thousands of tiny hairs that trap minute particles of water on the leaf surface. Nature uses all the methods at her disposal, frequently combining more than one in a single plant.

With so many clues to guide the gardener, it quickly becomes simple to select the plants more likely to succeed in hot, dry areas. A wide range of plants is adapted to thrive in full sun, including shrubs, perennials, bulbs, annuals and biennials; what follows is just a small selection of my favourites. If you look out for plants with the tell-tale signs of drought tolerance, you will discover a wealth of equally beautiful alternatives.

Achillea 'Terracotta' Plants come and go in popularity and achilleas are currently in the ascendancy. In recent years many new varieties have been introduced, offering a wide spectrum of colour to the gardener. They are relatively short-lived perennials that nonetheless warrant replanting. Their attractive, often grey-green, ferny foliage is joined by flattened flower-heads from midsummer to early autumn, each one composed of dozens of tiny flowers. In *Achillea* 'Terracotta' these are a warm burnt orange, fading to pale tangerine as they mature. Both colours are seen on the plant simultaneously, with new flowers opening as others begin to age.

Achilleas work beautifully with the new perennial planting style that is characterized by naturalistic combinations planted in informal drifts. Position them so that they create a swathe of colour running through grasses and clumps of daisy-like rudbeckias or echinaceas. The feathery leaves add softness, while the flattened shape of the flower-heads provides a useful horizontal accent that serves to break up a sea of vertical stems, foliage and flowers. Many achilleas need dividing and replanting to keep them flowering and have a tendency to give up the ghost altogether, but the unusual shape of their densely packed flower-heads and extensive range of glowing colours make them invaluable plants for the sunny border and well worth a little extra effort.

Achillea 'Terracotta'
COMMON NAME Yarrow
HARDINESS Fully hardy
ZONE 3
HEIGHT 75cm (2½ft)
SPREAD 60cm (2ft)
CULTIVATION Moderately fertile, well-drained soil. Full sun.
OTHER VARIETIES *Achillea* 'Lachsschönheit' – salmon pink flowers, which fade to a pretty combination of cream and pale pink. *A.* 'Martina' – a sturdy new variety with creamy yellow flowers. *A.* 'Summerwine' – a glamorous, deep burgundy red form.

Anthemis tinctoria 'Sauce Hollandaise'

The pretty flowers of this perennial are packed with cheerfulness and simply make me feel happy. An abundance of daisy-shaped blooms smother the plant throughout the summer, each golden centre surrounded by rays of pale creamy yellow, a colour that is accurately captured by its name. The flowers rise on slender, branching stems high above the finely cut, dark green, basal foliage. They are produced in profusion, with new buds opening in steady succession, so that a single clump will be smothered with gently swaying flowers for many weeks.

I find this plant invaluable in the mixed or herbaceous border: it brightens a monotonous colour scheme and adds lightness to more structural neighbouring plants. Its pale creamy tones associate well with a wide range of other colours – particularly flowers in the blue and mauve spectrum – and the subtle shade is easier to place than strident whites. As summer nears its end, the clump of stems may become a bit untidy and can be cut right back to the base. This is a no-nonsense plant, whose jolly flowers and feathery foliage offer really good garden value. Be sure to grow enough for cutting, as the flowers bring the essence of summer to an informal arrangement.

Anthemis tinctoria 'Sauce Hollandaise'
COMMON NAME Dyer's chamomile
HARDINESS Fully hardy
ZONE 4
HEIGHT 60cm (24in)
SPREAD 40–60cm (16–24in)
CULTIVATION Moderately fertile, sandy, well-drained soil. Full sun.

Iris pallida subsp. pallida I adore irises and selecting just one from the vast range of colours and sizes available is far from easy. In the end I opted for the simple perfection of one of my long-time favourites, the species *Iris pallida* subsp. *pallida* – one of the ancestors of all hybridized bearded irises. Its flowers are flawless, with elegant standards and well-balanced falls in a pure, clear shade of lavender-blue; in the throat of each fall is a softly hairy, white beard or crest that is tipped with gold. Best of all is their unexpectedly intense fragrance. This rhizomatous iris has no need of modern improvements like ruffled petals and bizarre colour combinations; it succeeds by not trying too hard.

Up to six flowers are borne on the upper section of the tall stems. When in bud, each flower is enrobed in a papery, silver sheath, which peels open to reveal the tightly furled, indigo petals of the juvenile blooms. The foliage is almost as good as the flowers: a fan of slender, grey-green blades, whose clean lines continue to look good in the border long after the flowers have faded. Their vertical shape sets off the flowers beautifully and provides a strongly architectural element within the general planting scheme. As with all irises, the flowers – although breathtaking – are all too fleeting, so is it worth growing nonetheless? The answer is a resounding 'yes'.

Iris pallida subsp. *pallida*
HARDINESS Fully hardy
ZONE 4
HEIGHT 90cm (3ft)
SPREAD 60cm (2ft)
CULTIVATION Fertile, humus-rich, well-drained soil. Full sun.

Perovskia 'Blue Spire' With sprays of misty mauve flowers and pale silvery foliage and stems, this is a wonderful plant for a border in full sun. Perovskia is beautiful grown en masse and I've seen it used most effectively as tall, informal edging on either side of a path, the individual plants merging to form clouds of tiny flowers. These appear in mid- to late summer and last through to early autumn. They work beautifully with the full spectrum of blue and lilac-flowered planting partners and blend well with other pastel shades.

I love this plant for its softening qualities; the hazy profusion of flowers is light and airy and the colour of both flowers and foliage gives a sense of coolness to hot, dry areas. *Perovskia* 'Blue Spire' is similar in tone to some of the paler lavenders and, like them, it has aromatic foliage: indeed, the distinctive scent gives rise to its common name, Russian sage. Perovskia is a low-maintenance subshrub: simply cut all the stems close to ground level in early spring and the new growth, which should already be emerging, will quickly reach its full height and spread. The narrow, silver-grey foliage is a sure sign of adaptation to dry conditions, so it will cope well with hot summers and should not need watering once it is established.

Perovskia 'Blue Spire'
COMMON NAME Russian sage
HARDINESS Fully hardy
ZONE 5
HEIGHT 1.2m (4ft)
SPREAD 1m (3ft)
CULTIVATION Moderately fertile, well-drained soil. Full sun.

Artemisia 'Powis Castle'

The more I work with plants, the more I appreciate the contribution that foliage makes to a successful garden. You can create an attractive planting scheme without flowers, but not without beautiful leaves. Among the most useful and sought-after leaf colours is silver and this plant provides some of the best silver-grey foliage. Not only is the colour lovely, but the individual leaves are prettily shaped and subtly aromatic. Each finely dissected leaf looks like a piece of filigree lace and massed together they produce a billowing, cloud-like effect.

This perennial forms a permanent woody base, but in our climate it can look very sorry for itself after a long winter and benefits from hard pruning in the spring. It soon puts on new growth, yet retains a compact shape. I find *Artemisia* 'Powis Castle' invaluable for the front of the border, where its silver tones work beautifully with all pastel shades. It is a particularly good foil to the full spectrum of blues, lilacs, pinks and white. The pale, luminous quality of its foliage brings light to the front of the border and the deeply cut, feathery texture of its leaves softens any planting scheme.

Artemisia 'Powis Castle'
COMMON NAME Wormwood
HARDINESS Frost hardy
ZONE 6
HEIGHT 60cm (2ft)
SPREAD 90cm (3ft)
CULTIVATION Moderately fertile, well-drained soil. Full sun.

Eryngium × oliverianum

The public imagination really seems to have been captured by this unusual perennial. At gardening shows I frequently see its distinctive flowers bobbing above the top of a carrier bag and nurserymen confirm that it sells like hot cakes. Part of its appeal lies in its strongly architectural shape. Branching stems rise from a clump of toothed foliage at the base of the plant and further leaves cling to the stems, each one marked with white veining and tipped with a sharp spine. Each branch of the stem ends in a cone-shaped flower surrounded by a collar of spiky bracts. Both stems and bracts are a luminous steely-blue – a hue of hypnotic beauty.

Eryngiums are invaluable for bringing structure to the border in the form of intricately jagged shapes. They contrast well with softly billowing perennials and flowing grasses, and are complemented by silver-grey foliage plants. Grow them in the midst of a mixed or herbaceous border or give them plenty of space and a stark backdrop of gravel for a more dramatic effect. They are also perfectly suited to growing in seaside conditions as they thrive in thin, sandy soil and stand up well to a battering from salt winds and rain. I have also admired them in a sleekly modern setting, growing alongside grasses with a metallic sheen and the aggressive-looking *Agave americana* in a garden composed of galvanised metal and mirrored surfaces.

Eryngium × oliverianum
HARDINESS Fully hardy
ZONE 5
HEIGHT 90cm (3ft)
SPREAD 45cm (18in)
CULTIVATION Moderately fertile, well-drained soil. Full sun.

Papaver rhoeas 'Mother of Pearl' Who could resist the sheer prettiness of these ethereal annual poppies? 'Mother of Pearl' is a cultivated form of the common corn poppy that is found growing wild throughout Europe and beyond and is a strain of the popular Shirley poppy. It was selected for the subtle nuances of its misty pastel shades with colours that range from dusky pink and mauve to pale lilac and a smoky dove grey. The petals may be flecked with little streaks in a darker shade or edged with a different tint. The flowers – which are carried on slender, hairy stems – are usually single, but semi-doubles are regularly thrown up, their translucent petals unfurling like crumpled tissue paper.

Seed should be sown where it is to flower in either autumn or spring. The mix of colours may vary from one seed company to another and from packet to packet; occasionally stronger tones of scarlet and orange will appear and should be pulled up, unless you like the effect. Thread a seam of seeds through a sunny border or scatter them randomly onto a gravel garden where they will germinate in the gaps between the stones. The flowers are undoubtedly fleeting and a heavy downpour will knock the petals off, but perhaps the ephemeral nature of these poppies adds to the feeling that one must seize the moment of flowering and enjoy it to the full.

Papaver rhoeas
 'Mother of Pearl'
COMMON NAME
 Corn poppy
HARDINESS Fully hardy
ZONE 5
HEIGHT 90cm (3ft)
SPREAD 30cm (12in)
CULTIVATION Fertile, well-
 drained soil. Full sun.

Sedum 'Ruby Glow' Sedums are an extraordinary group of plants, ranging from small, ground-hugging mats of foliage to bold, leggy specimens. All of them are ideally suited to life in the sun, with fleshy, succulent foliage that helps to conserve precious water. *Sedum* 'Ruby Glow' is one of the best. It forms a low-growing mound of thick, juicy green leaves with a hint of purple at the edges that are attached to sinuous red stems. In midsummer, a multitude of star-shaped flowers begins to open from tiny, pointed, dark pink buds. The colour deepens as they open fully to smother the plant in a glowing cloak of ruby red that lasts well into autumn. The clusters of flowers are so abundant that all one sees from a distance is an undulating cushion of velvety crimson.

This reliable, deciduous perennial can be grown in a mixed border providing the soil has sufficient drainage. However, I prefer to see it growing through gravel, an arid backdrop that sets off the highly decorative stems, leaves and flowers to best advantage. Sedums provide a welcome burst of colour towards the end of the season when many flowering plants can be looking a bit tired. Grow it in front of dark-stemmed dahlias and between clumps of the strap-like leaves and arching flowers of montbretia. It also associates well with many of the warmer-toned grasses, such as *Stipa arundinacea*, providing a contrasting solidity to the fluid movement of the grass.

Sedum 'Ruby Glow'
COMMON NAME Ice plant
HARDINESS Fully hardy
ZONE 4
HEIGHT 25cm (10in)
SPREAD 45cm (18in)
CULTIVATION Fertile, well-drained soil. Full sun.
OTHER VARIETIES *Sedum spathulifolium* 'Cape Blanco' — a ground-hugging mat of pale, silvery leaves, with yellow flowers. *S. spectabile* 'Iceberg' — pale green, fleshy foliage and white, star-shaped flowers. *S. telephium* subsp. *maximum* 'Atropurpureum' — deep purple stems and foliage and tiny pink flowers.

Knautia macedonica This perennial is justifiably a stalwart in the planting schemes of many a garden designer. Each plant forms a basal clump of soft green foliage, through which long, skinny stems appear, each one branching into an even narrower stem topped with a flower resembling a scabious. These blooms are exceptionally long-lasting and, at their peak in mid- to late summer, a profusion of compact, nodding flowers dances above the leaves and mingles with neighbouring perennials. The pretty, pincushion blooms are a rich, ruby red – a colour currently at the height of horticultural fashion and much seen at the Chelsea Flower Show in recent years.

Knautia macedonica is a perfect mixer plant: its subtle qualities enable it to be positioned between two neighbouring plants that don't quite sit comfortably together and successfully blend and blur the edges between the two. The tall, airy stems bring transparency to the border and lightness to a plant that might otherwise have a more sombre quality, given the intense crimson of its flowers. This combination of delicacy and depth, informality and gravitas, endows this plant with an innate elegance that explains its rising popularity.

Knautia macedonica
HARDINESS Fully hardy
ZONE 5
HEIGHT 60–80cm (24–32in)
SPREAD 45cm (18in)
CULTIVATION Moderately fertile, well-drained soil. Full sun.

autumn leaf colour

As a child, autumn was my favourite time of year – I remember the pleasure of walking through piles of fallen leaves, kicking them into the air with every step. Autumn is still a special time for me; it is a season to be looked forward to, rather than a bleak ending to the gardening year. Just as Guy Fawkes Night approaches, so the 'fireworks' of the plant world prepare to go off with a bang.

Many different factors combine to affect the quality of autumn colour in any given year. Weather, temperature and soil conditions can all have a bearing on the depth and brilliance of the colours. Annual variations aside, some plants require a specific soil type – or direct sun in order to produce their most vivid tints; others are far less fussy, effortlessly and reliably displaying a symphony of colour.

What appears to be a magical display for our benefit is nature's way of shutting down deciduous plants for the winter. As temperatures drop and the day shortens, any remaining resources stored within the leaves are withdrawn and conserved for the following year, after which the foliage drops. The colours change as a direct result of the withdrawal of the green pigment chlorophyll, from the leaves.

The range of both strong and subtle hues encapsulated within autumn leaves is breathtaking, from pale butter yellow and gold to tangerine orange and scarlet, while reds can be as varied as ruby and crimson, deep plums and purples and the russet tones of bronze and copper. The most dramatic effects are achieved by combining several plants of contrasting tints together, to create a scene as rich and intricate as a tapestry. Combining trees, shrubs and perennials of different heights and shapes will produce pyrotechnics of the most exuberant kind.

Alternatively, choose a single stunning specimen and give it a backdrop of dark-leaved evergreens. With the colour at its peak it will form a solid block of a single shade, shouting its presence in the warm sunshine of an autumn garden. This use of restraint and simplicity can prove more startling and effective than a multi-coloured scene – a classic example of less is more.

The texture and shape of a leaf is emphasised by the addition of autumn colouring: lumps and bumps stand out in sharp relief on the surface of a mottled leaf. The area either side of the veins is often last to change colour, creating vivid contrasts of tone and an exquisite pattern of intricate tracery. Foliage that was merely interesting becomes breathtaking and every detail is picked out.

The transient nature of dazzling autumn colour is a great part of its appeal. You cannot expect to capture something so beautiful and ephemeral, and the inescapable fact that it will never again appear quite the same is somehow reassuring. Seize the moment, look long and hard, commit the view to memory, take a photograph – for the resplendent scene you see today may be gone tomorrow.

Geranium wlassovianum

Good autumn colour is usually associated with shrubs and trees, but there are several perennials that deliver the same effect. Among the best is *Geranium wlassovianum*, a native of China, Mongolia and eastern Siberia, which produces pretty, dark-veined, magenta-purple flowers from mid summer to early autumn. These rise above a clump of softly hairy, dark green foliage, tinged with a hint of deep bronze. The leaves have an attractive rounded shape and deeply cut edges that form an intricate outline.

As autumn approaches the mature foliage begins to colour; the leaf edges turn first, with the veins retaining their green colouring for longest. Gradually the entire surface changes to shades of scarlet, crimson, orange and golden yellow, becoming deep purple before finally fading. Meanwhile, juvenile green leaves continue to be produced until the end of the season, so that the overlapping foliage creates a tapestry of glorious tints, before dying down completely as winter approaches.

This is a lovely geranium to combine with late summer and autumn-flowering perennials for a flash of brilliant, late-season colour. Group several plants together to create a large swathe, or dot individuals among neighbouring plants towards the front of a border. However you choose to grow it, *G. wlassovianum* merits much more recognition; it provides interest from the moment it emerges, until its dazzling climax in a cacophony of colour.

Geranium wlassovianum
COMMON NAME Cranesbill
HARDINESS Fully hardy
ZONE 5
HEIGHT 60cm (2ft)
SPREAD 60cm (2ft)
CULTIVATION Moderately fertile, moist but well-drained soil.
  Full sun to partial shade.

Acer palmatum 'Ôsakazuki'

I'm mad about Japanese maples. My smallish, urban garden contains no fewer than nine acers, some grown as feature plants in pots and others dotted around both the front and back gardens. I love their graceful forms and beautifully shaped leaves, but for sheer, show-stopping autumn colour acers are hard to beat. The foliage of *A. palmatum* 'Ôsakazuki' is among the very best in a strong field: its young leaves are dark green, but as autumn nears they turn orange and scarlet, their rich shades becoming increasingly intense until they peak in a glowing ruby red. In a group of autumnal trees and shrubs, this acer is invariably the one that stands out like a beacon.

This variety grows tall enough to be described as a small tree rather than a shrub, but acers are relatively slow-growing so it will take some time to reach its full height. Acers thrive in dappled shade, but you should choose a sheltered spot because exposure to strong winds can damage their delicate foliage. Pruning is unnecessary: in fact, it is far better to select a position that will give your plant plenty of growing room and allow its elegant framework to develop naturally. A graceful habit, stunning autumn colour and low maintenance requirements give this Japanese maple undoubted star quality.

Acer palmatum 'Ôsakazuki'

COMMON NAME Japanese maple
HARDINESS Fully hardy
ZONE 6
HEIGHT 6m (20ft)
SPREAD 6m (20ft)
CULTIVATION Moist but well-drained soil. Sun to partial shade.
OTHER VARIETIES *Acer palmatum* 'Beni-shidare' – dome-shaped shrub whose dissected, lacy, bronze foliage becomes scarlet in the autumn. *A. palmatum* 'Seiryû' – with an upright growth habit, its finely cut, green foliage takes on gold and scarlet autumn tints. *A. palmatum* 'Sango-kaku' – coral red stems and apple green foliage with red tints to the edges. The leaves colour butter yellow in autumn.

Cornus sanguinea 'Winter Beauty' Although best known for its appeal in winter, this deciduous dogwood surpasses itself in terms of year-round garden-worthiness; and justifies its inclusion in this chapter by virtue of its autumn colour. Shrubby dogwoods are grown predominantly for their attractive summer foliage and colourful bare winter stems; *Cornus sanguinea* 'Winter Beauty' not only fulfils these requirements, but goes on to score a bonus with good autumn tints. Its leaves unfurl mid-green in spring, and as autumn approaches they begin to turn butter yellow and pale tangerine before falling – a respite from the hot reds of many autumnal leaves. What remains is even more colourful: a clump of strongly vertical, naked stems in shades of gold, orange and scarlet.

All but the smallest gardens should be able to accommodate the neat habit of this lovely shrub. In order to encourage the production of new stems – which will have the most vivid colouring – cut out about two thirds of the older stems to within 5–10cm (2–4in) of ground level in early spring. I generally avoid removing all the growth in one go, which can be unnecessarily stressful for the plant, and follow the pruning with a generous mulch of organic material to give it a boost. For maximum impact position at least three shrubs together – preferably more. The result will be a swathe of brilliantly glowing stems, that shines brightly in the winter sun.

Cornus sanguinea
'Winter Beauty'
COMMON NAME
 Common dogwood
HARDINESS Fully hardy
ZONE 4
HEIGHT 3m (10ft)
SPREAD 2.5m (8ft)
CULTIVATION Tolerant of
 most soils. Full sun.

Crataegus persimilis 'Prunifolia' Visit the Royal Botanic Gardens, Kew, during the autumn, and there in all its splendour you will find a magnificent, mature specimen of one of my favourite trees, *Crataegus persimilis* 'Prunifolia'. The lower branches of its rounded crown, which reach almost to the ground, are cloaked in spectacular autumn colour. The richness of the effect is heightened by prolific quantities of scarlet berries, which follow white flowers in early summer.

Although this tree takes some time to achieve the stature of the example at Kew, it does cry out for a bit of space. It never becomes very tall and would be best described as a small tree, but the canopy eventually spreads widely. So it is not suitable for a small garden. It looks its best grown as a single specimen in a position where you can walk around it and admire it from all sides.

From the shape of the foliage it would be hard to recognise this tree as a member of the hawthorn family. Throughout spring and summer the glossy rounded leaves are dark green, in autumn they begin to colour gradually, the green mingling with dark bronze and plum shades. As the season progresses, the foliage brightens, taking on gold, orange and scarlet tints, and forming a compact, dome-shaped mass of glorious colour.

Crataegus persimilis
  'Prunifolia'
COMMON NAME
  Plum-leaved hawthorn
HARDINESS Fully hardy
ZONE 3
HEIGHT 8m (26ft)
SPREAD 10m (33ft)
CULTIVATION Tolerant of
  most soils. Full sun.

Cotinus 'Flame' Several members of the *Cotinus* genus are worthy candidates for inclusion in this chapter. One of my favourites is *C.* 'Flame', a large vigorous, deciduous shrub, or small tree that amply earns the space it takes up in the garden. The splendour of its autumn colouring is merely a delightful bonus for a shrub with such a long period of appeal. The young, rounded leaves are a fresh green in spring and summer, when they form a backdrop for the plumes of flowering inflorescences, that give rise to its common name of smoke bush. Airy clusters of pink flowers form a cloud-like haze, enveloping the entire shrub so that from a distance it appears to be in soft focus.

The froth of flowers is followed in autumn by a spectacular display of brilliant orange and scarlet tints. The colours glow like warm embers, brightening even the dullest day. This is a wonderful specimen shrub for a small to medium-sized garden, where it can be allowed to develop into a bushy tree. In a large garden it will become one of the highlights of a shrubbery, woodland area or substantial mixed border. Maintenance requirements are low: no pruning is required, other than removing dead wood, and it will thrive on ordinary unfertilised soil – too rich a diet may actually inhibit the intensity of its autumn colours.

Cotinus 'Flame'

COMMON NAME Smoke bush/tree

HARDINESS Fully hardy

ZONE 5

HEIGHT 6m (20ft)

SPREAD 5m (16ft)

CULTIVATION Moderately fertile, moist but well-drained soil. Full sun to partial shade.

OTHER VARIETIES *Cotinus coggygria* 'Royal Purple' – deep plum-purple leaves in spring and summer are followed by crimson autumn colour. *C.* 'Grace' – this vigorous form has claret-coloured foliage, which turns scarlet in autumn, and deep pink flowers.

Liquidambar styraciflua 'Worplesdon'

In an inspired and unusual example of urban street planting, the trees lining the road outside my house are not the routine limes or sycamores but an avenue of *Liquidambar styraciflua*. Local residents and I look forward all year to a spectacular display of autumn colour. 'Worplesdon' is a particularly attractive form, with maple-like leaves divided into long slender individual lobes, often with jagged edges. Throughout spring and summer they are dark green, but in autumn they deepen to shades of purple, orange and yellow before falling – with foliage in all these colours remaining on the tree simultaneously. Plant it in full sun to ensure the most intense hues.

This is a special tree worthy of a prime position in a medium-sized or large garden. Its silhouette is compact and shapely, with well-balanced, upright, sweeping branches, that open out with age. Although it can be grown in a woodland setting, I think it needs to be given plenty of space in order to be admired from all sides, as it glows like a torch in the warm sunshine of an Indian summer's day. If you are looking for a statuesque specimen tree with excellent autumn tints, this will fit the bill perfectly. Alternatively, the straightforward species *L. styraciflua*, has slightly broader leaves and good autumn colour, while the equally impressive *L. styraciflua* 'Lane Roberts' turns to rich, dark shades of aubergine and deep crimson.

Liquidambar styraciflua 'Worplesdon'

COMMON NAME Sweet gum
HARDINESS Fully hardy
ZONE 5
HEIGHT 25m (80ft)
SPREAD 12m (40ft)
CULTIVATION Fertile, moist but well-drained soil. Full sun.

Euonymus alatus

Euonymus alatus This attractive deciduous shrub really comes into its own in autumn, when it reliably delivers excellent colour. The simply shaped, dark green leaves, which are paired up along the stems, undergo a metamorphosis to become one of the most striking sights in the autumn garden. They colour beautifully to a rich shade of pinkish crimson – a hue of startling intensity – and droop rather elegantly from the spreading stems before fluttering to the ground. The shrub's other distinctive feature is its bark; corky ridges which form elongated wings along the surface of the stems and branches.

In addition to the vivid leaf colour, clusters of dangling, ruby berries add to the decorative effect. Its slow growth and useful medium size make this shrub a welcome addition to the smaller garden, where it will become a dominant feature in autumn. Grow it as a single specimen in a mixed border or combine with other shrubs – evergreens will form a backdrop for the red foliage, while selected deciduous shrubs with yellow, orange or scarlet tints can be used to create a blaze of colour. Equally good are *Euonymus alatus* 'Compactus', a dwarf form that is suitable for low hedging, and *E. alatus* var. *apterus* (pictured), a less common variety that lacks the winged bark, but is every bit as dazzling in terms of colour.

Euonymus alatus

COMMON NAME Winged spindle tree
HARDINESS Fully hardy
ZONE 5
HEIGHT 2m (6½ft)
SPREAD 3m (10ft)
CULTIVATION Tolerant of most soils. Sun or shade.

Vitis 'Brant' Climbers rarely come to mind when thinking of autumn colour, yet some of the most dazzling tints are found in members of the vine family. *Vitis* 'Brant' is an ornamental grapevine that becomes woody at the base and climbs by means of twining tendrils. It is densely covered with bright green leaves, which are divided into three or five lobes to form the distinctive vine-leaf shape. In autumn the foliage turns gradually to crimson and bronze; the veining remains green while the rest of the leaf surface glows ruby red. This creates a sharp contrast until the colours merge and become deep gold shortly before the leaves brown and fall.

Accompanying the autumn leaf colour are bunches of small grapes that are black with a dusky grey bloom – these are edible and are often surprisingly tasty. This fast-growing climber is best suited to a large expanse of wall or fence – a sunny spot will produce the best colouring. Its vigorous growth can be kept under control with judicious winter pruning; by restricting the vine in this way, you can also grow it over a pergola or trellis arch. With large, handsome leaves and intense autumn colour, this is a knockout foliage plant of considerable stature.

Vitis 'Brant'

COMMON NAME Ornamental grapevine
HARDINESS Fully hardy
ZONE 5
HEIGHT 7m (21ft)
CULTIVATION Moderately fertile, moist but well-drained soil. Full sun to partial sun.
OTHER VARIETIES *Vitis coignetiae* – the dark green, textured foliage of this extremely vigorous climber takes on brilliant scarlet autumn hues. *V. vinifera* 'Purpurea' – its maroon leaves with a silver-grey tinge turn deeper shades of plummy purple in autumn.

shade-loving perennials

Some of my favourite plants are shade-lovers. In fact, if I didn't have any shade in the garden I'd have to create some in order to grow them. Thankfully I have a fair amount, as do the vast majority of gardeners. Indeed, those of us with city gardens may have more than our fair share, with high walls, towering street trees and neighbouring buildings creating some very dark corners. Yet, the more experienced I become as a gardener, the more I am drawn to the infinite variety of the plants that dwell in the shadows.

It's important to remember that there are different types and degrees of shade, from the dry shade beneath the canopy of large conifers to the lightly dappled shadows created by airy, deciduous shrubs and trees. Sometimes a section of the garden will be in full sun during the morning only to fall into complete shade in the afternoon, or be permanently dark and damp near a wooded stream.

Whatever the type of shade in your garden, there are plants adapted to cope with it. Select the right plant for the conditions and the results will be spectacular. Some of these will be shrubs, which create the permanent, structural framework of the garden. With these in place you can embroider and embellish with perennials.

Many shade-loving plants have small flowers. It makes sense, as there's little point in wasting energy on showy blooms where pollinating insects and birds are less likely to spot you. It's far better to opt for another attractant, such as scent, which is often exceptionally good in some of these tiny flowers. Their colours are often muted too, with white and pale pastels showing up far better in low light, where they glow beautifully. The result is subtlety: shade is not the place for garish hues, but for lilac, pale pink, deep maroon and above all, white, the perfect palette for creating the most elegant planting schemes.

What these cool customers lack in flower colour, they more than compensate for with a startling range of leaf colour, texture and shape. Take advantage of this bounty and aim to select a variety of contrasting foliage and stems. Deep purple and bronze, vivid acid-green and yellow, and the full range of greens from palest apple to dark emerald are represented, as are several types of variegation. Only narrow, silver foliage is absent from the panoply of shade-loving plants.

Don't forget the touchy-feely aspect: textures range from smooth and glossy to rough and knobbly. It's all about choosing interesting combinations and being bold with your planting. Above all, enjoy the darker areas of your garden; why struggle with wrongly positioned sun-lovers when plants that thrive in shade have so much to offer? The shady garden has an enduring quality that surpasses the more obvious charms of show-stopping blooms and gaudy annuals and there is no reason why it shouldn't be the loveliest of all.

Alchemilla mollis Lady's mantle is among the most consistently reliable and best-loved hardy perennials and its ability to thrive in sun or shade adds to its value in the garden. Grown for both foliage and flowers, it has an attractive, low-growing, mound-forming habit. The rounded leaves have a softly felted surface created by hundreds of minute hairs that trap moisture so that after rain each leaf is studded with tiny droplets of water glistening like mercury.

In early summer, masses of tiny, sulphurous yellow-green flowers create a vibrant, frothy haze. Their colour combines well with most companion plants, complementing soft pink roses, contrasting with purple salvias, and brightening shady corners of the border.

There are endless uses for lady's mantle. Edge the front of a border and allow the flowers to spill over the path, dot it between hostas, heucherellas and geraniums wherever there are gaps in a shady border, or for maximum impact group plants together in a large swathe within the confines of a low, clipped, box hedge. Be assured that it will seed around freely if the flowers are not removed as soon as they start to fade. Cutting the entire plant back will prevent this and encourage a second flush of young foliage. However, you may prefer to encourage the young seedlings and develop a garden with the unkempt essence of English country style.

Alchemilla mollis
COMMON NAME
  Lady's mantle
HARDINESS Fully hardy
ZONE 4
HEIGHT 50cm (20in)
SPREAD 50cm (20in)
CULTIVATION Fertile, moist
  but well-drained soil.
  Sun to partial shade.

Milium effusum 'Aureum'

Shady borders can look a bit gloomy if the foliage is a repetitive sea of mid-green. What they need is a little variety and something to brighten up the scene. Bowles' golden grass does the trick nicely, with tufts of bright yellow-green, slender leaves. The foliage has a softness that allows the top of the vertical growth to arch over. In mild areas, the semi-evergreen leaves remain through the winter, but can look rather bedraggled in bad weather. In late spring, needle-thin stems carry airy spikes of tiny flowers that glisten after rain with minute droplets of water.

The bright colour is a real asset, contrasting beautifully with a wide variety of flowers and foliage. Perhaps the best combinations are with blues or purples; mauve-flowered columbines and the violet-blue *Geranium* Rozanne are perfect partners, but the humble forget-me-not is hard to beat. For the best effect, plant in a bold group, as a solitary plant will make little impact. Although it is not a long-lived perennial, if the conditions are right Bowles' golden grass is a prolific self-seeder: in my garden I find little tufted seedlings turning up in nearby pots, cracks in the paving and throughout the border.

Milium effusum 'Aureum'

COMMON NAME Bowles' golden grass
HARDINESS Fully hardy
ZONE 5
HEIGHT 60cm (2ft)
SPREAD 30cm (12in)
CULTIVATION Humus-rich, moist but well-drained soil.
  Partial shade.

Euphorbia amygdaloides 'Craigieburn'

I first became acquainted with this excellent spurge while filming at *BBC Gardeners' World Live* in Birmingham. I was scouring the stands for choice specimens with which to fill a show garden when I was offered half a dozen large pots of an extraordinary euphorbia. It was love at first sight and we haven't looked back.

Euphorbias are among my favourite groups of plants and there are many lovely examples, but not all of them have good shade tolerance. This particular wood spurge has a sturdy disposition with stocky stems in a rich shade of burgundy. Arranged along the length of the stems are whorls of foliage. The youngest leaves at the top are a glowing claret-red, fading to dark green as they age.

In mid-spring, bright acid-green flowering clusters open at the tips of the stems. Nestling among the ruby-coloured foliage, with the darker, mature leaves as a backdrop, the vivid yellow-green provides an exciting colour contrast. As the flowers open fully, the clusters enlarge dramatically, putting on a marvellous display until early summer. For the best effect, group several plants together in dappled shade, with yellow-green grasses and the purple-leaved *Actaea simplex* (Atropurpurea Group) 'Brunette' for company. As with all euphorbias, avoid contact with the sap, which can be a skin irritant.

*Euphorbia
  amygdaloides
  'Craigieburn'*
COMMON NAME
  Wood spurge
HARDINESS Fully hardy
ZONE 6
HEIGHT 50–60cm (20–24in)
SPREAD 60cm (24in)
CULTIVATION Moderately
  fertile, moist but well-
  drained soil. Partial shade.
OTHER VARIETIES *Euphorbia
  amygdaloides* 'Purpurea' –
  toned down alternative
  with similar colouring but
  smaller flowering cymes.
  E. amygdaloides var.
  robbiae – vigorous variety
  with a subtle rosy blush to
  the young foliage and less
  showy flowers.

Anemone × hybrida 'Honorine Jobert'

Any plant that flowers in the no man's land of late summer is welcome and one that does so in sun or shade becomes a treasure. This Japanese anemone offers so much: an attractive clump of foliage that is well developed by late spring, from which rise tall, sturdy stems, giving valuable height to a planting scheme. The icing on the cake are the comparatively small flowers that appear from tight, round buds on the tips of the stems as summer nears its close, and last well into mid-autumn. The flowers have wonderfully open, rounded faces of snowy white petals, with a ring of golden yellow stamens encircling a bright green centre. They have all the charm of a daisy, yet far more sophistication.

The pure white flowers work beautifully in dappled shade, where their pale tones reflect the low light and glow like beacons from a backdrop of foliage. Individual plants dotted through the border will sway elegantly above their low-growing companions, but if you have the space I'd certainly recommend planting en masse, as there are few sights as spectacular as a swathe of flower-topped stems gently nodding in the breeze. Wherever I've seen them grown in this way, they have taken my breath away.

Anemone × hybrida 'Honorine Jobert'
COMMON NAME Japanese anemone/windflower
HARDINESS Fully hardy
ZONE 5
HEIGHT 1.2–1.5m (4–5ft)
SPREAD 50cm (20in)
CULTIVATION Fertile, humus-rich, moist soil. Sun to partial shade.
OTHER VARIETIES *Anemone × hybrida* 'Königin Charlotte' – large, pink, semi-double flowers on a tall, sturdy plant. *A. × hybrida* 'Elegans' – elegant, single, pink flowers that gradually pale as they age. *A. × hybrida* 'Whirlwind' – whorls of pure white petals in semi-double flowers.

Rodgersia podophylla

I love the effects that can be created with foliage alone: the contrasts of texture and colour are often more decorative than flowers. This clump-forming perennial is an archetypal foliage plant for shade. It grows beautifully under a canopy of trees in a certain Mr Titchmarsh's garden, where it is planted in a large swathe with pale green shuttlecock ferns for company.

The leaves are large at about 40cm (16in) across and have an attractive, palmate shape with jagged edges. They are purple-bronze when young, becoming green through the summer, before turning red-bronze in the autumn. With so much beauty in the foliage, the flowers seem almost unnecessary and I know gardeners who remove them altogether. Nevertheless, the tall, airy stems of tiny, cream flowers are attractive and add height through the summer, so I prefer to keep them.

This plant provides excellent ground cover and a strong architectural shape. When used in a large group, the effect is of a lush sea of foliage through which no soil can be seen. It makes an excellent backdrop for the flowers of bleeding heart, columbine and hellebores, and is perfect interplanted with early spring-flowering bulbs, whose dying foliage will be hidden by its spreading leaves. The delicate foliage of astilbes, actaeas and a whole range of ferns provides a wonderful contrast to this invaluable gentle giant of the border.

Rodgersia podophylla

HARDINESS Fully hardy
ZONE 5
HEIGHT 1.5m (5ft)
SPREAD 1.8m (6ft)
CULTIVATION Moist, humus-rich soil. Sun to partial shade.
OTHER VARIETIES *Rodgersia aesculifolia* – mid-green foliage reminiscent of horse-chestnut leaves with tall flowering stems in white or pink. *R. pinnata* 'Superba' – heavily veined, palmate leaves, purple-bronze when young, and panicles of deep pink flowers.

Dicentra spectabilis 'Alba' As a child, this was one of my favourite plants; who could fail to be captivated by its charms? One of the earliest heralds of warmer weather, in sheltered gardens the foliage is already well advanced by early March. These leaves are extremely decorative in their own right, a fresh, light green with pretty, fern-like, lacy shapes, but it's the flowers, which appear at the beginning of April and last until the end of the spring, that I really look forward to.

The way the flowers are held on the plant is particularly enchanting. They are suspended from long, slender stems, which arch gracefully under the weight of their dangling treasure. The individual flowers hang on delicate stalks and each one looks like a tiny heart or, if you invert it, a bathing figure, similarities that give rise to their common names of Bleeding heart and Lady in the bath.

Most of us are familiar with the sugar-pink colouring of *Dicentra spectabilis*, but I prefer the more subtle beauty of the white form. A row of little, snow-white hearts trembling in the breeze has such a pure and endearing appeal. This is an invaluable plant for early spring interest in my north-facing border, where it is accompanied by clumps of *Helleborus* × *hybridus* and *Corydalis solida*. Don't be fooled by its dainty appearance: this is a tough, easy-going plant for shady places.

Dicentra spectabilis 'Alba'
COMMON NAME Bleeding heart/
 Lady in the bath
HARDINESS Fully hardy
ZONE 3
HEIGHT 1.2m (4ft)
SPREAD 45cm (18in)
CULTIVATION Fertile, humus-rich, moist soil.
 Partial shade.

Geranium phaeum 'Samobor' Many hardy geraniums will tolerate a degree of shade, but my favourite, *Geranium phaeum* 'Samobor', is an unassuming plant that rewards closer inspection. Foremost among its many attributes are the leaves, which are attractively lobed and marked with a distinctive, central stain of deep purple-bronze. From a generous basal clump of foliage rise slender stems that reach about 70cm (28in) tall and on which the leaves gradually decrease in size towards the top.

The small flowers are usually arranged in pairs on fine branching stalks and, although understated, are exceptionally beautiful. They have a richly saturated, deep burgundy colour, with a simple, flattened arrangement of petals and prominent stamens. The flowering stems sway in the breeze, mingling with those of neighbouring plants, and in my sheltered garden they look gorgeous from mid-April until early June. Once the flowers have faded, I cut the stems right to the base, which encourages new foliage to appear, and the leaves continue to make a decorative contribution to the border.

This isn't a showy plant, as the dusky colour can make the flowers hard to spot from a distance, but I prefer to have some quiet plants in the garden, which require a little effort to discover and enjoy. This is an excellent plant for the front of a shady border or a woodland planting scheme and I cannot recommend it too highly.

Geranium phaeum 'Samobor'
COMMON NAME
 Dusky cranesbill
HARDINESS Fully hardy
ZONE 4
HEIGHT 60–80cm (2–2.5ft)
SPREAD 45cm (18in)
CULTIVATION Moderately
 fertile, moist but well-
 drained soil. Sun to
 partial shade.
OTHER VARIETIES *Geranium phaeum* 'Album' — bears snowy white flowers that show up well in shade. *G. macrorrhizum* 'Ingwersen's Variety' — makes good ground cover with pretty, pink flowers.

Hosta undulata var. albomarginata

I grow many hostas in my shady town garden and this is the most reliable. It's invariably the first to appear, sending up shoots of tightly furled leaves by mid-March. By contrast, it is generally the last to be eaten: the slugs and snails gorge themselves on the leaves of other varieties, leaving this one untouched. Even by the end of the summer it looks relatively unscathed, while its neighbours have often been reduced to lacy skeletons.

Hostas are invaluable perennials for shade, adding structure and lush foliage in a wide range of colours, shapes and sizes. Forming a mound of overlapping, mid-green leaves with creamy white margins, this variety performs brilliantly as ground cover beneath deciduous shrubs and trees, yet looks equally lovely on the front edge of a shady border or at the base of a wall. It may not be the most glamorous hosta, but it makes a useful foil for other plants and its variegation adds a touch of brightness to a dark corner.

As with most hostas, the pale lilac flowers are held on tall stems well above the foliage. Cut them down as they begin to fade and continue to enjoy the leaves until they turn yellow in the autumn. By all means try one of the many methods of slug and snail control, but be assured, you will have a better chance of success with this hosta than with most.

Hosta undulata var. albomarginata

COMMON NAME Plantain lily
HARDINESS Fully hardy
ZONE 3
HEIGHT 55cm (22in)
SPREAD 60cm (24in)
CULTIVATION Fertile, moist but well-drained soil.
  Partial to full shade.
OTHER VARIETIES *Hosta* 'Halcyon' – elegant classic with
  glaucous blue-green colouring. *H.* 'June' – a real beauty
  patterned with tones of blue-green, mid-green and apple-green
  on one leaf. *H.* 'Night before Christmas' – colour-contrasted
  leaves with pale cream centres and dark green edges.

Helleborus × hybridus

The winter garden becomes a more exciting place if it includes a selection of *Helleborus × hybridus*. The subtly beautiful flowers appear from mid-winter onwards and last for months. Their palette ranges from pure white and cream through various shades of pink to maroon so deep that it almost appears dusky black. The permutations are made even more varied by the highly individual markings on the petals: some are speckled or tinged with green. Other hybrids have double and anemone-centred blooms, many of which are breathtakingly beautiful.

Because each hellebore is unique, the best way to acquire them is to visit a specialist nursery at flowering time to select your personal favourites. Look out, too, for some of the more recently bred strains with upright-facing flowers, although to me half the fun is tipping up the flower to discover its hidden beauty. In a couple of years your newly planted hellebore will bulk up to form a neat clump that can be divided shortly after flowering to create further new plants, and they are also prolific self-seeders.

Hellebores are generally trouble-free perennials, thriving in the humus-rich soil beneath deciduous shrubs and trees. They can occasionally be susceptible to blackspot and it's best to remove any affected leaves to prevent it spreading further. In any case, you may prefer to remove old foliage when it looks tatty by cutting it back to the base: fresh, new leaves will appear shortly after the flowers emerge.

Helleborus × hybridus
COMMON NAME Lenten rose
HARDINESS Fully hardy
ZONE 4
HEIGHT 45cm (18in)
SPREAD 45cm (18in)
CULTIVATION Fertile, humus-rich, moist but well-drained soil. Partial shade.

Corydalis flexuosa 'Purple Leaf'

There are certain plants I always look out for as signs that spring is well on the way. By early March, this corydalis' distinctive, neat mound of lacy foliage is already in place. The foliage is a treasure in itself: beautifully dissected leaves tinged with tones of deep purplish-red. A month or so later the crowning glory appears: a mass of small flowers that captivates year after year. These long-lasting blooms are an extraordinary shade of blue with a hint of violet, an electric shade rarely seen in plants. Their elongated shape with little spurs is no less unusual and the flowers appear to dance above the foliage in the slightest breeze, moving like a shoal of miniature tropical fish.

It's sometimes said that corydalis is difficult to grow, but in my experience this couldn't be further from the truth. In my garden it thrives on neglect, needing no upkeep whatsoever, and now into its fourth year, it continues to delight. A spot at the front of a shady or semi-shaded border and an annual mulch with leaf-mould is all it requires. There are various named forms such as *C. flexuosa* 'China Blue', which has clear turquoise flowers. However, corydalis have often been mis-named and there is some confusion over the individual forms. The best way to be sure of getting a plant you like is to visit a nursery or garden centre when the plants are in flower.

Corydalis flexuosa 'Purple Leaf'

HARDINESS Fully hardy
ZONE 4
HEIGHT 30cm (12in)
SPREAD 20cm (8in)
CULTIVATION Moderately fertile, humus-rich, moist but well-drained soil. Partial shade.

transparent plants

The loveliest views in the garden are multi-layered and have a sense of mystery. To achieve this look one needs to juxtapose and overlap plants, some of which, for the best effects, should be see-through. Of course no plant is literally see-through, but transparency can be achieved using plants that form airy screens. This chapter celebrates the voile curtains of the plant world.

When I started learning how to put plants together, the advice was somewhat rigid and oversimplified, and until recently the use of planting in contemporary garden design had become increasingly hard-edged, and often secondary to the structural landscaping. Happily, a new and overwhelming trend towards more naturalistic planting schemes has now arrived, blowing like a breath of fresh air through the garden.

I have been fascinated for some time by finding ways to loosen up the border, experimenting with planting combinations in which flowering perennials are dotted among grasses to give a random effect – although in practice they are often carefully placed. Suddenly, ranks of identical perennials planted in solid blocks of threes, fives or sevens look terribly dated.

The softness and femininity that are the hallmarks of this recent trend are wonderfully liberating. One of the most successful ways of achieving the look is to layer plants of different heights, using tall specimens at the front to break up the more familiar, formal, banked-up system of strictly height-regimented planting combinations. The most effective groupings work when the plants nearest the front provide height without solidity. Tall but transparent plants can weave a diaphanous web of lacy flowers over their sturdy, but shorter, neighbours. Sheer curtains of seed-heads shimmer in low sunlight, while clusters of tiny flowers create a hazy froth of hovering petals.

Transparent plants need not mean minute flowers. Many plants with see-through characteristics consist of reasonably large flower-heads atop long, slender stems. The effect is the same: a tall, airy plant in the foreground breaking up the view of something more substantial planted behind, adding to its value in the garden and sharpening the eye. At first sight the background plant is seen in conjunction with the see-through plant in front, with vistas and patterns created through a network of stems and branches, the colours blending or contrasting. As the viewer moves round, the plant further away comes into plain sight, giving another chance to experience its beauty.

Several perennials fall into the category of see-through plants once they send up their flowering stems. They may have clumps of basal leaves or diminutive foliage on the stems, but these stems are for the most part exceptionally skinny, which gives the required delicacy. A single transparent plant will soften any planting combination, but the ultimate effect is achieved when groups of ethereal plants are grown together. From a distance a mist of hazy shapes and colours appear to blend and merge. The slightest breeze whips the stems and seed-heads into a blur of movement and the garden takes on a dreamlike quality.

Dierama pulcherrimum

(Opposite) I was first captivated by this plant at the Garden House in Buckland Monachorum, Devon, where it sways gracefully in a colourful sea of California poppies, Livingstone daisies and Million Bells petunias, in a scene of breathtaking beauty. Its elegant, arching stems, tipped with clusters of pendulous, magenta, bell-shaped flowers, give rise to its evocative common name of angel's fishing rod. The stems stand above an evergreen clump of grass-like foliage, and the flowers dangle from needle-fine stalks throughout the summer.

A native of southern Africa, it will appreciate a sunny spot with really well-drained soil for its underground corm. Often planted in association with water, it looks equally good punctuating the corner or curve of a bed, or growing up through gravel in a more arid setting, where it will often self-seed.

This is a plant that needs some air around it to look its best; cluttering the surrounding space with tall-growing perennials will cramp its style and detract from the elegance of its form. However, give it the company of low-growing, drought-tolerant annuals, which can be seen through the slender stems, and you will have a winning combination.

Dierama pulcherrimum
COMMON NAME
  Angel's fishing rod
HARDINESS Frost hardy
ZONE 7
HEIGHT 1–1.5m (3–5ft)
SPREAD 60cm (2ft)
CULTIVATION Fertile, humus-
  rich, moist but well-
  drained soil. Full sun.

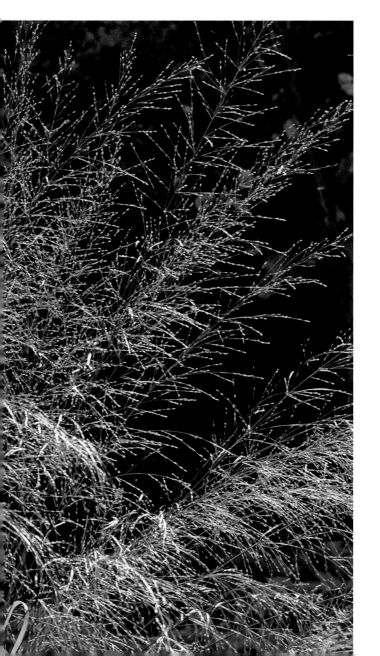

Molinia caerulea subsp. arundinacea 'Transparent'

Of the many grasses that could qualify for inclusion in this chapter, this is perhaps the most aptly named. A low-growing clump of foliage is crowned from late spring to early winter by slender, gently arching stems up to 2m (6½ft) tall topped with trembling, open panicles of delicate flowers. From a distance the effect is of a gossamer fine cloud; when a breeze moves the stems, they waft gently, while a stronger wind whips them into an effervescent froth. After light summer rain, tiny droplets of water cling to the inflorescences and sparkle.

To get the best from this irresistibly tactile grass position it near the front of the border, ideally on a corner or curve where it has plenty of room to shine. Alternatively, group it in bold swathes and enjoy the effect en masse. Either way, for all its gauzy delicacy, this is a grass with plenty of impact. Unlike many grasses, members of the *Molinia* genus rarely look attractive once winter really sets in and the end of November is a good time to chop them down to the base and look forward to the following year's new growth.

Molinia caerulea subsp. arundinacea 'Transparent'
COMMON NAME Purple moor grass
HARDINESS Fully hardy
ZONE 5
HEIGHT 2m (6ft)
SPREAD 1.8m (6ft)
CULTIVATION Humus-rich, moist but well-
  drained, preferably neutral to acid soil.
  Partial shade.

OTHER VARIETIES *Molinia caerulea* subsp. *arundinacea* 'Karl Foerster' – popular form with arching stems and open, airy flowers. *M. caerulea* subsp. *arundinacea* 'Skyracer' – stiff, upright-growing and, above all, tall stems make this the perfect choice for a vertical accent. *M. caerulea* subsp. *arundinacea* 'Windspiel' – upright cultivar with substantial-looking panicles of flowers.

Cephalaria gigantea The giant scabious is a gentle beast of a plant with an unkempt appearance
that is perfect for the looser planting styles currently popular. It is incredibly tall, reaching 2.4m (8ft)
when in flower, and has a myriad of stems that are stout at the base, becoming more slender as
they reach for the sky. Their ends are topped with flowers during early summer. The flowers are
disproportionately small, opening from button-like buds to a very pretty scabious shape in palest
lemon yellow. The foliage is also very attractive: delicate and well proportioned.

This is an easy-going, clump-forming perennial; despite its enormous height, the stems shouldn't
need support and during the autumn when the plant starts to look tatty they simply need to be chopped
right back to the base. Most books will recommend you plant *Cephalaria gigantea* at the back of the
border, but I've seen it used most successfully towards the front, creating interesting combinations with
the other plants that can be spied through gaps in the stems. It also combines extremely well with
naturalistic wildflower plantings. If you're looking for a little drama in the garden, here is proof that you
can get maximum height in the border without using overbearing, opaque plants.

Cephalaria gigantea
COMMON NAME
   Giant scabious
HARDINESS Fully hardy
ZONE 3
HEIGHT 2.5m (8ft)
SPREAD 60cm (2ft)
CULTIVATION Moderately
   fertile, moist but well-
   drained soil. Full sun.

Crambe cordifolia Appearing at first to be a shrubby froth of pure
white flowers, this is in fact a clump-forming perennial of considerable
substance, reaching well over 2m (6½ft) in height and spread at its peak.
From late spring to midsummer a mound of large, rounded, dark green
leaves is crowned by a multitude of dainty, individual flowers. These
inflorescences are produced en masse on a vast framework of narrow,
branching stems. The tiny flowers are sweetly scented – some might say
cloying – and highly attractive to bees. From a distance, when in full bloom
the clouds of snowy white flowers resemble lightly whipped candyfloss.

This is an easy plant to grow, given good drainage at the roots and
sufficient shelter from strong winds which would otherwise decimate the
flowers. Although it mixes well with most perennials, *Crambe cordifolia*
looks particularly stunning against a backdrop of contrasting foliage as part
of a cool, white border. It will also thrive growing through gravel with self-
seeded annuals for company and associates well with grasses. If you don't
deadhead once the flowers have faded, in warmer areas you'll be rewarded
with decorative seed capsules for the remaining summer and autumn.

Crambe cordifolia
HARDINESS Fully hardy
ZONE 6
HEIGHT 2.5m (8ft)
SPREAD 1.5m (5ft)
CULTIVATION Fertile, humus-rich, well-drained soil. Full sun.

Verbena bonariensis

Verbena bonariensis This may be one of the most fashionable plants of recent years, but plants only become really popular when they have real merit and *Verbena bonariensis* is no exception. Clusters of tiny, mauve flowers are borne on the tips of extremely slim stems, which are stiffly upright with small, toothed leaves and an open, branching habit. This gives plenty of air around each cluster of flowers and a good view through the criss-crossing mesh of stems. Looked at closely, each individual flower is lovely, but packed together they have more impact and intensity of colour.

This archetypal see-through plant exemplifies how valuable transparency can be and there are few styles of garden that would not benefit from its inclusion. It looks wonderful planted in a vast swathe or dotted throughout the border among shorter perennials, where it will continue to look good from midsummer through to the autumn. A native of South America, it also works beautifully when grown through gravel, towering over drought-resistant sowings of annual poppies and daisies. It is a short-lived perennial, but if the flowers are left to set seed they sow themselves around happily, turning up in the most unexpected places.

Verbena bonariensis
HARDINESS Frost hardy to fully hardy
ZONE 9
HEIGHT 2m (6½ft)
SPREAD 45cm (18in)
CULTIVATION Moderately fertile, moist but well-drained soil. Full sun.

Thalictrum delavayi

Meadow rue has many excellent qualities and, although its charms are subtle, it always attracts attention. When in flower it provides a diaphanous, see-through effect in shadier areas of the garden. The ideal position would be in partial shade with plenty of moisture, where you'll be rewarded by a host of droplet-shaped buds that open into small, pinky-mauve flowers with cream-coloured stamens, a combination that resembles the pale colours of vanilla and raspberry ice-cream. Each tiny flower is suspended from a needle-thin stalk at the tips of a tall network of slender stems that are tinged with purple. The effect, which lasts from midsummer into early autumn, is ethereal.

As with the other plants in this chapter, the effect relies not on a single flower, but on the appearance of many small flowers produced all together. In this case, the airy panicles of flowers are the icing on the cake for a plant with extremely pretty foliage. The leaves are deeply divided, giving an elegant, ferny effect that adds to the plant's contribution before and after flowering. To keep them looking their best, the tall flowering stems may need staking, particularly if there are no neighbouring plants to support them.

Thalictrum delavayi
COMMON NAME Chinese meadow rue
HARDINESS Fully hardy
ZONE 5
HEIGHT 1.2m (4ft)
SPREAD 60cm (2ft)
CULTIVATION Moist, humus-rich soil. Partial shade.
OTHER VARIETIES *Thalictrum delavayi* 'Album' – choose this form for a cool, hazy effect from panicles of pure white flowers. *Thalictrum delavayi* 'Hewitt's Double' – the long-lasting, tiny, double flowers dispense with cream stamens and are a single tone of mauve.

Stipa gigantea An archetypal see-through plant, this beautiful grass is key to achieving the layered look. It gives structure with lightness, and impact with delicacy. In summer, tall flowering stems tower over clumps of evergreen or semi-evergreen foliage, the oat-like seed-heads trembling with the slightest movement. These flowering panicles have a purple-green tinge when young, ripening to pale gold, hence its common name of golden oats. Their airy construction, with each individual seed hanging from a thread-like stem, gives *Stipa gigantea* incredible grace and elegance.

Given a position with space to be seen from all sides, this grass is quite spectacular back-lit on a summer evening, creating a golden halo of shimmering seed-heads. I've seen it used most successfully on the front corner of a border, where it is impossible to walk by without stroking the seed-heads. Alternatively, several specimens positioned in a row create a sheer curtain with height and impact. This is an effective way to divide sections of the garden without the heaviness and opacity of a more solid hedging plant. Don't be tempted to cut down the stems during the autumn tidy-up: if you leave them in situ, they will sparkle on frosty mornings and give a ghostly quality to the border.

Stipa gigantea
COMMON NAME Golden oats
HARDINESS Fully hardy
ZONE 7
HEIGHT 2.5m (8ft)
SPREAD 1.2m (4ft)
CULTIVATION Moderately fertile, moist but well-drained soil. Full sun.

Sanguisorba officinalis

Some plants qualify for see-through status by virtue of the compactness of their flowers and the thinness of their stems, rather than an overall airy quality. The great burnet is one such plant. Each narrow stem ends in what appears to be a single, dark burgundy-red, toggle-shaped flower, but is in fact neatly made up of dozens of minute, individual flowers. These miniature bottlebrushes appear from early summer to mid-autumn and there is such a proliferation of red-tinged stems that the plentiful flowers appear to be scattered among neighbouring plants.

Found in the wild in wet meadows and near streams, this lovely plant needs moist conditions in partial shade to thrive. Early in the season the foliage forms an attractive mound of small, oblong leaves, from which the flowering stems will appear. Both the foliage and the bobbing flowers combine well with solid-looking shade-lovers such as hostas and heucheras, whose leaves contrast in size and colour. This is not a plant for lovers of tidy gardens: the stems rarely stand to attention and may flop over their shorter neighbours without some support. However, its dishevelled appearance is a brilliant foil for more substantial companion plants and its loose habit brings a naturalistic disorder to the border.

Sanguisorba officinalis
COMMON NAME Great burnet
HARDINESS Fully hardy
ZONE 4
HEIGHT 1.2m (4ft)
SPREAD 60cm (2ft)
CULTIVATION Fertile, humus-rich, moist soil. Sun to partial shade.

roses for scent

Everyone has their desert island plants – the ones they can't imagine gardening without – and mine would have to be roses. Few plants offer such beautiful flowers, over such a long period, with such breathtaking fragrance. The scent of the rose is renowned world-wide and throughout history mankind has made strenuous efforts to capture its essence in expensive oils and exclusive perfumes. The range of fragrances is outstanding: myrrh, tea, old rose and musk are but a few of the evocative names used to describe them. Gardening is a multi-sensory experience; colour, texture, shape and form combining with scent in a complex series of layers to create a satisfying whole. Roses are valuable additions in many ways, but for me, no matter how beautiful it looks, a rose without perfume is never quite complete.

Scent is a very personal pleasure; it can be evocative, romantic, calming, or invigorating. Everyone's reaction to a fragrance is highly subjective; each person interprets the same scent differently and men and women rarely respond in the same way to a single bloom – one claiming it is highly perfumed, while the other is unable to smell it at all. The intensity of the fragrance can also be affected by the time of day, temperature, age of the flower and many other factors. The important thing is to please yourself and grow what works for you. Position scented roses where you can get the full benefit of the fragrance. Grow climbers on the wall behind a seat or near a door, and group shrubs toward the front of the border within sniffing range.

Roses may have romantic connotations, but they are also incredibly robust and versatile plants. Highly desirable qualities like disease-resistance and repeat flowering are uppermost in the minds of rose breeders and the quality and performance of plants is improving all the time. The overly complicated business of pruning has recently become de-mystified: trials have shown that plants given a quick going-over with a hedgetrimmer performed even better than those laboured over with a pair of secateurs. Modern improvements are a boon to the gardener, but don't neglect the older varieties; even a single flush of flowers is sufficient to justify a particularly beautiful rose. I find that good garden housekeeping – picking up and destroying leaves affected with black spot and using environmentally friendly methods of pest control – keeps the worst of the nasties under control.

Call me old fashioned, but I like to use roses wherever possible. Modern garden design seems to have largely ignored the rose, preferring architectural foliage plants and eschewing overly floriferous shrubs, but flowers – and in particular roses – are more than the quintessential ingredient in a typical English garden: they can be equally valuable in the twenty-first century garden. Choose your variety carefully and use colour sparingly, and the effect will enhance even the most contemporary space. Some roses cope admirably with shade and with varieties suitable for the border, walls, pillars, patios, containers and ground cover, there is something for every garden.

Rosa 'Compassion' This climber has a graceful name, but its constitution is far from delicate.
The first thing that struck me was the strength and thickness of its stems: sturdy, vertical growth covered with glossy, mid-green foliage and just a smattering of thorns. All that vigour is apparent in the flowers too: the large blooms are carried singly or in clusters of three or more on upright stems that are well able to support their weight. Repeating consistently throughout the summer and into autumn, the double flowers have a good shape, with gently curving petals filling each flower.

The rich coral-pink colour is strongest in the centre of the bloom, with paler apricot outer petals flushed with salmon-pink. As the flowers age they fade to a soft shell-pink, adding subtle nuances to the overall effect. The buds are particularly pretty, with intensely coloured, tightly furled petals, whose shades of apricot and coral-pink are reminiscent of the skin of a ripe peach. Its scent is more than a match for the strong visual appeal: an arresting combination of sweetness with a hint of lemon. Its compact size and strong growth makes this a perfect choice for a wall, pillar or fence in the smaller garden. Wherever it grows this is a rose with substance and staying power; the excellent perfume is just the icing on the cake.

Rosa 'Compassion'
HARDINESS Fully hardy
ZONE 5
HEIGHT 3m (10ft)
SPREAD 2.5m (8ft)
CULTIVATION Moderately
   fertile, humus-rich, moist
   but well-drained soil.
   Full sun.

Rosa 'Felicia' You would expect to find this pretty rose in a long forgotten rose garden as it has charm and femininity by the barrow-load. Despite its old rose appearance, this shrub rose was raised in 1928, making it a comparative youngster. An abundance of small, mid-green leaves provides the backdrop for the plentiful clusters of flowers. The individual blooms are small, opening from perfect little buds into softly shaped, double blooms that droop elegantly from slender stalks. Their colour is a subtle shell pink that is darker towards the centre and as they age they fade to pale pink with a hint of peach. Although small in size, each bloom packs a fragrant punch. The scent is strong and aromatic – the legacy of a distant, musk rose ancestry.

This is a vigorous rose with strongly spreading, bushy growth. It looks best planted in groups of three or more and needs plenty of room to give its best. Several plants positioned in a row will combine to make a substantial hedge for an informal garden. Ideally suited to cottage or country style, it can be used successfully in urban gardens to create the same languid and slightly ungroomed effect, with a continuous display of flowers from summer to autumn.

Rosa 'Felicia'
HARDINESS Fully hardy
ZONE 5
HEIGHT 1.5m (5ft)
SPREAD 2.2m (7ft)
CULTIVATION Moderately fertile, humus-rich, moist but well-drained soil. Full sun.

Rosa 'Königin von Dänemark' Old roses have so much to offer the modern gardener. They bring with them a host of romantic connotations and embody the spirit of an age when what mattered in a rose was the glory of a perfect bloom and heavenly perfume. This Alba shrub was raised in Germany in 1816 and has a rather lax, open shape with matt, grey-green leaves and a multitude of hair-like thorns on the young stems. The fully double, quartered, rosette-like flowers are of medium size and crammed with concentric circles of beautifully arranged petals. The centre of each flower is a deep rose-pink, with the outer petals softening to shades of light pink imbued with a hint of blue, fading on mature blooms to pale lilac-pink.

The flowers open from tiny buds borne in clusters on the end of the stems in one, glorious, mid-summer display. Their scent has been described as 'very strong', but I find it rather delicate, fresh and rosy. Cut generous trusses of this pretty rose and combine it with sprays of lady's mantle, *Alchemilla mollis*, for an informal table arrangement that will perfume the room. Our current preoccupation with repeat flowering should not blind you to the appeal of this lovely rose. Like a home-grown strawberry, when in season it's so good that you don't mind the wait.

Rosa 'Königin von Dänemark'
HARDINESS Fully hardy
ZONE 4
HEIGHT 1.5m (5ft)
SPREAD 1.2m (4ft)
CULTIVATION Moderately fertile, humus-rich, moist but well-drained soil. Full sun.

Rosa 'Roseraie de l'Haÿ' This is a rose with presence and staying power; hybridised more than a hundred years ago, it has passed the test of time. It's a big, sturdy grower with thorny stems and healthy, bright green, pleated leaves that have a tactile texture too often absent in other roses. The double flowers are a knockout, with a luminous magenta colour, a squashy informal shape and outstanding scent. Don't bother pushing your nose into the rose: just stand back and let the rich, sweet perfume come to you. After a main flush of flowers in early June, further blooms continue to delight throughout the summer.

Even from a distance this is one of the most instantly recognisable of all shrub roses. I spotted it while filming at the historic garden at Levens Hall in Cumbria, where several large specimens punctuate both sides of the hot-coloured borders. The head gardener, Chris Crowder, is happy to sing its praises, calling it 'bug proof'. This distinctive offspring of *R. rugosa* is certainly remarkably free of mildew and black spot and, given the choice, aphids seem to prefer other varieties. If you generally spray your roses, you can chuck out the spray gun with this one. For me, however, all these undoubtedly admirable qualities come second to its sheer beauty; I'd grow it even if the bugs loved it too.

Rosa 'Roseraie de l'Haÿ'
HARDINESS Fully hardy
ZONE 4
HEIGHT 2.2m (7ft)
SPREAD 2m (6ft)
CULTIVATION Moderately fertile, humus-rich, moist but well-drained soil. Full sun.

Rosa Gertrude Jekyll This English rose has become a modern classic. Small, pretty buds unfurl to reveal large, open rosettes of double, cupped flowers that are packed with petals. It's hard to believe that so much flower could be contained within such a little bud. The blooms are a rich, deep pink – a good strong shade to combine or contrast with purple-flowered and silver-leafed companions. Although the flowers have all the characteristics of an old rose, they are produced with regularity throughout summer and well into autumn, set off by large, grey-green leaves.

With a strong, upright habit, the tall, vigorous stems of this shrub rose are best positioned towards the back of the border where their lanky lower growth will be hidden behind other plants. This rose also performs well if treated as a compact climber, grown against a wall or fence or trained around a pillar or over an arch. This is a quality rose with scent to match. Its pervading perfume could be described as a quintessential old rose fragrance, intense and intoxicating. It seems appropriate that a rose of such stature should be named after one of the giants of gardening in twentieth century Britain, herself a renowned admirer of beautiful roses.

Rosa **Gertrude Jekyll**
HARDINESS Fully hardy
ZONE 5
HEIGHT 1.5m (5ft)
SPREAD 1m (3ft)

CULTIVATION Moderately fertile, humus-rich, moist but well-drained soil. Full sun.

Rosa Margaret Merril If elegance is what you're after, look no further. This floribunda rose is a cool customer with strong, compact growth and double, snowy white, urn-shaped flowers. As the blooms mature, their wavy-edged, rounded petals take on the merest hint of a pale pink blush and open fully to produce a goblet shape that flaunts a central ring of maroon and golden stamens. The flowers – which are generally carried in clusters of three or more – are set off beautifully by extremely dark green, leathery leaves. This dramatic foliage provides a strong contrast with the pure white, swirling petals, which remind me of whipped cream.

The flowers are produced in profusion throughout the summer and well into autumn and have good weather resistance, standing up well to the vagaries of the British climate. The sweetness of their strong scent is enlivened with a hint of spicy citrus. *R.* Margaret Merril would look very chic planted en masse inside a border of low, box hedging or as part of an all-white border. It is also an excellent variety for cutting, lasting well in the vase. Perhaps its only drawback is a susceptibility to blackspot, but in every other respect this is a very classy rose.

Rosa **Margaret Merril**
HARDINESS Fully hardy
ZONE 5
HEIGHT 75cm (2½ft)
SPREAD 60cm (2ft)
CULTIVATION Moderately fertile, humus-rich, moist but well-drained soil. Full sun.

Rosa 'Souvenir du Docteur Jamain'

Discovering this rose was the start of a love affair for me. Although it's been in cultivation since 1865, I first saw it at a recent Chelsea Flower Show adorning a trellis arch on the stand of one of the major rose growers. It was tall, dark and handsome and attracted plenty of attention from the admiring crowd: I too was soon hooked and ordered a plant immediately. The velvety, deep red flowers change to darker shades of burgundy and regal purple as they mature on the stems, finally becoming almost black. They are not large at a maximum of 7cm (2¾in) across, but they are beautifully formed with an abundance of soft petals. The scent is equally impressive: a rich, sweet perfume with a warmth that reflects the sultry appearance of the flowers.

This rose is perfect trained onto trellis or through an obelisk where it can reach up to 3m (10ft). To get the very best from it, choose a shady spot, rather than the bright sun of a south-facing position. The petals have a tendency to burn in strong sunlight – which will also cause the flowers to fade – they retain their intensity of colour far better in semi-shade. Sadly, as with many older varieties it doesn't have the disease resistance of modern cultivars, but if this rose were a wine, it would be a fine, aromatic, vintage claret and, with a succession of flowers, its beauty can be savoured for many weeks.

Rosa 'Souvenir du Docteur Jamain'
HARDINESS Fully hardy
ZONE 5
HEIGHT 3m (10ft)
SPREAD 2m (6½ft)
CULTIVATION Moderately fertile, humus-rich, moist but
  well-drained soil. Partial shade.

Rosa Graham Thomas

I grow a lot of roses in my garden, each of them beautiful in their own way, but Graham Thomas is in a class of its own. Its list of qualities begins with a sturdy framework and healthy, mid-green foliage. The flowers, which often appear in clusters of three or more, are beautifully shaped like an open goblet filled with rounded petals that are perfectly arranged around the centre. Their scent is a subtle, tea rose fragrance and is fresh, rather than overpowering. However, their chief asset is their colour, a rich golden-yellow with the intensity of an egg yolk that is unique to this rose. This shade is deepest on the inner petals of the younger flowers, fading to a paler warm yellow as they age.

The luminous golden colour of Graham Thomas works beautifully with blues and purples. I grow the stately *Delphinium* 'Faust' directly behind a group of three roses, where the electric violet-blue of the flowering spikes provides a wonderfully vibrant contrast. As with most shrub roses, you will achieve maximum impact if you plant them in groups of three or more; the individual plants will soon grow into one another to look like a single, large shrub. This rose is justifiably one of the most popular of David Austin's excellent English Roses, with all the charm of an old rose, strong, disease-resistant growth and a plethora of beautiful blooms throughout the summer.

Rosa Graham Thomas

HARDINESS Fully hardy
ZONE 5
HEIGHT 1.2m (4ft)
SPREAD 1.5m (5ft)
CULTIVATION Moderately fertile, humus-rich, moist but well-drained soil. Full sun.

trees for small gardens

Planting a tree is always an act of faith. For me, all the promise of the future is contained in a young sapling. In a small garden, the decision to plant a tree shouldn't be taken lightly, but I believe that a garden without a tree is often one without scale, stature and permanence. So small gardens need trees, but they must be the right ones. Take your time when deciding what to plant, because you will be living with your choice for a long time. If your garden is in a conservation area, remember that once a tree reaches a certain girth you will not be allowed to remove it without permission. The fact that you planted it won't carry any weight; this is planting for the long term.

Decide what you want the tree to do in terms of design. Do you want to hide an eyesore or block out the neighbours? Do you want heavy coverage or a transparent canopy of delicate foliage? What impact will the mature tree have on the light that currently reaches the garden and, of course, the house? All too often a slender sapling turns into a monster that blocks out the sun and plunges a once bright garden into gloomy darkness.

Practical considerations are more important when planting a tree than with any other plant. Are the roots likely to cause a problem with a wall, patio or foundations? You'll be able to underplant with shrubs, ground cover, bulbs and perennials while the tree is still young, but the range of suitable companion plants narrows as the tree gets larger and the surrounding soil becomes increasingly impoverished by its hungry and thirsty roots.

Getting the size right is vital. It's true that many trees will tolerate pruning if they outgrow their allotted space, but they develop a far better form if allowed to grow as nature intended. Choose a tree that will only grow to a size your garden can accommodate and don't underestimate how big it will get. Trees are genetically programmed to achieve a particular height and spread, so check what the likely size of a fully mature specimen will be, and be realistic about whether it will fit the space you have. The shape of the tree is also a deciding factor. In a truly tiny space, a narrow, columnar tree will be easiest to find a place for, it may grow tall it won't take up too much width. Trees of lesser stature may appear smaller, but often have a widely spreading canopy that fills the garden.

Few trees, if any, have all the attributes of blossom, attractive foliage, fruits or berries, decorative bark, autumn colour and elegant compact growth. However, a single tree in a small spot needs to earn its keep and to get the best value from it, choose a variety that gives you more than one season of interest. Try to see mature examples of possible candidates, ideally at different times through the year. Arboretums, public parks and gardens can all be sources of inspiration.

Sorbus vilmorinii This lovely tree is one that I recommend frequently for the smaller garden. Members of the rowan family are extremely elegant and this Chinese example is no exception. Beautiful foliage is generally the best asset of any tree and the delicate leaves of Sorbus vilmorinii, which consist of feather-like rows of dark green leaflets arranged along a central stem, are among the prettiest. In early autumn the fruits appear; these clusters of deep rosy-pink berries gradually fade almost to white as they ripen on the branches, retaining just a blush of pink. The fruits appear while the tree is still in leaf and last particularly well, resisting the attention of hungry birds until well into winter. Once the foliage starts to colour, it takes on attractive red and purple tints.

Despite their graceful appearance, rowans generally do well in tough conditions and are able to stand up to the wind and rain of exposed sites. Each leaf is made up of up to 30 narrow leaflets that allow strong winds to pass between them with little resistance, ensuring the stability of the tree. This easy-going tree is generally un-fussy in its requirements, and tolerates some shade. However, an open sunny position will produce the best leaf and berry colour.

Sorbus vilmorinii
COMMON NAME Rowan
HARDINESS Fully hardy
ZONE 6
HEIGHT 5m (15ft)
SPREAD 5m (15ft)
CULTIVATION Fertile, humus-rich, moist but well-drained soil. Full sun to partial shade.
OTHER VARIETIES *Sorbus cashmiriana* — an elegant airy habit, with pure white fruits which outlast the leaves. *S. commixta* 'Embley' — a stunning combination of orange-red berries and intense autumn leaf colour. *S.* 'Joseph Rock' — brilliant autumn tints and long-lasting, yellow fruits.

Pyrus salicifolia 'Pendula'

A flash of silver foliage can refresh any garden, brightening a repetitive rank of green-leaved plants. At first glance, it is easy to confuse this ornamental member of the pear family with a willow because of its long, slender leaves and weeping branches that swoop right down to the ground, forming a rounded cascade of shimmering foliage. Closer inspection reveals that the surface of each young leaf is covered in tiny, reflective hairs, which create the metallic sheen. As the foliage ages, it becomes a smoother, greyish-green before falling in the autumn.

Though it produces creamy white flowers in spring, followed by small pear-shaped fruits, the chief attractions of this useful small tree lie in its leaf colour and graceful growth habit. In addition to these virtues, it is tolerant of urban pollution, making it a good choice for a city garden, yet its somewhat unkempt appearance means that it works equally well in informal, country gardens. Use it to provide contrasting colour in the border or give it pride of place and plenty of space as a specimen tree in the lawn. Some people might argue that this tree becomes less inspiring in winter when its framework is bare of foliage, but for me its many plus points outweigh this drawback and, most importantly, there are few alternatives that offer such attractive colouring when in leaf.

Pyrus salicifolia 'Pendula'
COMMON NAME Weeping silver pear
HARDINESS Fully hardy
ZONE 4
HEIGHT 5m (15ft)
SPREAD 4m (13ft)
CULTIVATION Fertile, moist but well-drained soil. Full sun.

Betula utilis var. jacquemontii This birch has positive qualities in every season. Long catkins dangle from the slender branches in spring and the dark green leaves take on a golden yellow hue in the autumn, but by far its most startling attribute is its shimmering bark, which is a brilliant chalky white. It looks particularly beautiful when set against a dark background like a yew hedge, where the ghostly but elegant framework can be fully appreciated, particularly during the winter months.

Despite reaching up to 18m (60ft) in height, this tree qualifies for the small to medium-sized garden because its shape is more upright than broad and the leaf coverage is never dense. In common with many birches, it has an airy canopy that allows not only an under-planting of spring-flowering perennials and bulbs to thrive in the dappled shade created by its branches, but also a wide range of small shrubs with year-round interest.

There are several excellent named forms of this tree to look out for including 'Doorenbos' and 'Jermyns', but my favourite is 'Silver Shadow', which is a small variety with bark of dazzling purity. All make beautiful, single, specimen trees, although if you have a larger garden they are particularly lovely grown in a small group of three or more. Select either a single-stemmed tree or a multi-stemmed example to make the most of the decorative bark.

Betula utilis var.
  jacquemontii
COMMON NAME
  West Himalayan birch
HARDINESS Fully hardy
ZONE 5
HEIGHT 18m (60ft)
SPREAD 10m (33ft)
CULTIVATION Fertile, moist
  but well-drained soil.
  Full sun to partial shade.

Acer griseum The paper-bark maple is a beautiful small tree in every respect, with plenty to offer throughout the year. The delicate, dark green leaves of this Chinese native are composed of three leaflets and turn first to orange and then a rich crimson in autumn. However, for the chief glory of the tree look no further than the trunk and branches, which are covered with an unusual and highly distinctive bark that peels off in thin, papery sheets. Strips of the uppermost layer cling to the trunk like rolls of grated chocolate, exposing the cinnamon-coloured new bark beneath the rich, peeling flakes. Standing close to the tree, it's hard to resist pulling off the sections that are beginning to lift away.

A slow rate of growth ensures the tree doesn't suddenly get too big for its allotted space. However, as with many good things, the colouring and texture of the bark takes time to develop and improves with age, so don't be impatient with newly planted saplings, as their most distinctive characteristics will gradually appear. An attractive, broadly spreading shape and the exceptionally decorative bark make this a perfect winter-interest tree, but spring brings the addition of small, acid-yellow flowers, which are followed in turn by winged seed cases that pirouette as they're carried away on the wind.

Acer griseum
COMMON NAME Paper-bark maple
HARDINESS Fully hardy
ZONE 5

HEIGHT 10m (33ft)
SPREAD 10m (33ft)
CULTIVATION Fertile, moist but well-drained
  soil. Sun to partial shade.

Prunus 'Shôgetsu' This tree takes pride of place in my garden and deserves to be better known. I wanted a Japanese flowering cherry with show-stopping, blowsy blossom and good autumn leaf colour and I haven't been disappointed. The intense, sugary pink colours often associated with flowering cherries are not to my taste, so having done some homework I chose this variety for its pendulous clusters of double, white flowers that open from rosy-pink buds, creating a stunning combination. The blossom is accompanied by the new leaves, which unfurl a fresh green with serrated edges. When in full flower, the effect is a pure celebration of spring.

Despite having modest requirements in terms of cultivation, this tree certainly delivers the 'wow' factor. However, its flattened spreading crown, which can reach 8m (26ft) wide, makes it unsuitable for a very small garden and it's a shame to alter the natural form with pruning.

P. 'Shôgetsu' is one of the last cherries to come into flower, saving itself for mid- to late May. This was one of the main considerations for me; I wanted to enjoy the tree in good weather and the sight of a profusion of blossom against a clear, blue sky is breathtaking. Spring is undoubtedly the highlight: it's almost a bonus when in autumn the leaves turn to shades of coral, apricot and, finally, bronze before falling.

Prunus 'Shôgetsu'

COMMON NAME Japanese cherry
HARDINESS Fully hardy
ZONE 5
HEIGHT 5m (15ft)
SPREAD 8m (25ft)
CULTIVATION Moderately fertile, moist, well-drained soil. Full sun.
OTHER VARIETIES Prunus 'Pink Perfection' – double rose pink flowers accompanied by bronze young leaves, which unfurl bronze. P. 'Shirotae' – large, snow-white flowers and fresh green, young foliage combine to perfection. P. 'Umineko' – elegant goblet-shaped tree, with plentiful single, white flowers in early spring and beautiful autumn tints.

Prunus × subhirtella 'Autumnalis Rosea' When you are blessed with a small garden you soon learn to 'borrow' attractive plants from neighbouring plots. Just the other side of the brick wall that divides my garden from the one next door is a wonderful, autumn-flowering cherry, *Prunus × subhirtella* 'Autumnalis Rosea'. It completely fills the view from the upstairs window, creating a spectacular sight when in full bloom.

Its name rather misleadingly implies that flowering is confined to the autumn, whereas in fact the tree is sprinkled with delicate blooms during milder spells throughout the winter and I've even seen it in flower on Christmas Day. Blossom is especially welcome in the depths of winter when all around is looking drab and this tree gives us something to look forward to during the cold months.

The semi-double, palest blush-pink flowers are very tiny, so the effect is like a dusting of icing sugar, rather than a thick coating of gaudy flowers. The blossom appears on the bare branches or with the first leaves intermittently from November to March. In spring the mid-green foliage emerges fully and later takes on butter yellow and finally bronze hues before falling in the autumn. This tree will only reach up to 8m (25ft) high, but its spreading crown does need a reasonable amount of headroom. However, the small size of the individual leaves and the lightness of the canopy ensures that the effect is airy rather than dense and it's possible to underplant successfully with ground-covering shrubs and perennials.

Prunus × subhirtella
 'Autumnalis Rosea'
COMMON NAME
  Winter-flowering cherry
HARDINESS Fully hardy
ZONE 6
HEIGHT 7–8m (22–25ft)
SPREAD 8m (25ft)
CULTIVATION Moderately
  fertile, moist but well-
  drained soil. Full sun.

Gleditsia triacanthos 'Sunburst'

This tree is among the larger specimens in this section, but I include it because its open shape makes it suitable for all but the smallest plots and few trees offer such distinctive leaf colour. While in growth, the newly produced young leaves are a particularly vivid yellow-green, contrasting effectively with the darker green of the mature foliage. This splash of glowing colour brightens the garden brilliantly on even the dullest day. The leaves are also extremely pretty in shape – composed of fern-like individual leaflets on either side of a central spine and give the tree its distinctive and rather delicate appearance. Growth habit is also attractive, the horizontally held branches festooned with feathery foliage.

Unlike the straightforward species, *Gleditsia triacanthos*, this form has no frightening thorns on its stems, making it a more friendly addition to the family garden. The similar colouring and airy habit make it a good alternative to the more commonly planted *Robinia pseudoacacia* 'Frisia', which is prone to die-back in the lower branches. With a tough, easy-going disposition, good tolerance of urban pollution and wonderfully vibrant colouring, this tree is a reliable and cheerful asset to city and rural gardens alike.

Gleditsia triacanthos
 'Sunburst'
COMMON NAME
 Honey locust
HARDINESS Fully hardy
ZONE 5
HEIGHT 12m (40ft)
SPREAD 10m (33ft)
CULTIVATION Moderately
 fertile, moist but well-
 drained soil. Full sun.

Malus 'John Downie'

British gardeners have a real affection for apple trees, but the best choice for many gardens is an ornamental crab apple. If you're looking for spring blossom followed by edible fruits, look no further. The flowers, which appear in late spring, are pink in bud, opening to white. They are bunched in prolific clusters along the length of the stems and the crab apples that follow in autumn are equally plentiful. These highly decorative fruits are creamy yellow flushed with orange and scarlet and hang from long stalks, like ripe cherries. A particular feature is their attractive, elongated shape from stalk to base. The leaves are simple, but provide a good backdrop to the ornamental ebullience of the flowers and fruits.

Although the fruits make a dazzling display, the birds will help to ensure they don't last very long on the tree. It's best to enjoy the spectacle while you can and aim to harvest the fruits, which make excellent crab apple jelly, just before they fall. Dappled shade will do for this pretty tree, but it will flower and fruit better if you can position it in full sun. Although young trees have an upright shape, they will open out and broaden with age, so allow sufficient headroom when deciding where to plant.

Malus 'John Downie'
COMMON NAME Ornamental crab apple
HARDINESS Fully hardy
ZONE 3
HEIGHT 10m (33ft)
SPREAD 6m (20ft)
CULTIVATION Moderately fertile, moist but
 well-drained soil. Full sun to partial shade.

OTHER VARIETIES *Malus* 'Evereste' – an upright growth habit and an abundance of vivid orange-yellow fruits. *M.* × *robusta* 'Red Sentinel' – white blossom, followed by crimson fruits that stay on the tree well into winter. *M.* × *zumi* var. *calocarpa* 'Golden Hornet' – pure white blossom and clusters of golden-yellow fruits.

flowers with sultry colour

A riot of colour is all very well, but I am increasingly drawn to the stunning shades at the darker end of the spectrum. It would appear that I am not alone; award-winning show gardens at all the major flower shows have recently been packed with dusky foliage and stems, and flowers in sultry tones. Far from being melancholy, the seductive appeal of these exotic hues is timeless and they evoke a rare sense of mystery and passion. The garden benefits from areas of sombre subtlety that give the eye a break from a continuous stream of lively colours.

There is much talk of black or nearly black flowers, but in truth this colour is rarely found in plants. More often than not, the tones are a richly saturated red or purple and it is the complexity and subtlety of the shading that adds to their voluptuousness. The depth of colour is only half the story: many of the loveliest dark-toned flowers also owe their appeal to the texture of their petals.

The satin sheen of deep crimson tulips, the beetroot-stained, silk petals of opium poppies and the inky black tones of tiny violas make the hairs on the back of my neck stand up. In the same way that a crescendo in a piece of music creates an almost palpable 'electricity' in the auditorium, or an intense perfume makes you swoon, these colours – and the enhancing effect they have on the texture of a flower – are among life's great sensual experiences.

However, just as one dab of essential oil goes a long way, the richness of these intense shades needs to be handled with skill, and occasionally restraint. One approach is to devote an entire area to similar colours. By layering the different shapes and textural feel of flowers, leaves and stems in a continuous swathe of tone-on-tone planting, one maximises the impact of these glamorous plants.

The alternative is to treat them as highlights, planning with care the contrasting combinations that can be made with surrounding plants. Dark-toned flowers work beautifully with all the 'hot' colours – vivid scarlet *Crocosmia* 'Lucifer', deep crimson *Monarda* 'Prärienacht', orange *Dahlia* 'David Howard' and *Kniphofia* 'Bees' Sunset' would all make perfect companions to dark-flowered plants.

Luminous acid green is another excellent colour to contrast with plum and mulberry tones: the bright flowers of euphorbias and *Smyrnium perfoliatum* would certainly wake up these intoxicating shades, as would the arching leaves of *Hakonechloa macra* 'Aureola' or *Carex elata* 'Aurea'. Grasses in the warmer colour range make equally good partners and those with bronzed stems, foliage or flowerheads are particularly complementary.

Fashion may be as influential in gardening as in anything else, but I believe these mouth-watering, velvety colours have a lasting fascination that is beyond a mere fad. Their attraction is on a subliminal level and the contribution they make to the mood of the garden is indisputable. If gardening is now deemed to be 'sexy', the following plants are surely part of the reason why.

Alcea rosea 'Nigra' Some plants instantly evoke a specific setting or style and hollyhocks are inextricably linked with cottage gardens. However, this particular example brings with it a dramatic appeal far removed from the gentle pleasures of domestic country life. Its summer flowers, which open wide like a gramophone horn, have silky petals in a richly saturated shade of mulberry so deep that it appears almost black in low light. The throat of each bloom is golden yellow and the soft petals are often dusted with a sprinkling of contrasting pale yellow pollen. The flowers nestle among the small, pale green leaves that adorn the upper section of the towering stems, while towards the base of the plant the foliage becomes progressively larger.

Hollyhocks are notoriously susceptible to disfiguring hollyhock rust. Unless you are prepared to take preventative action by spraying the leaves with a fungicide throughout the season, I suggest you treat these perennials as biennials in order to limit the spread of the disease. A group of hollyhocks growing by a cottage door is a familiar image from dozens of soft-focus Victorian paintings portraying an apparently idyllic rural life. However, there is a place for them in a more contemporary garden: they add height and stature to the mixed border, and – in such luscious colours. – a touch of welcome glamour.

Alcea rosea 'Nigra'
COMMON NAME Hollyhock
HARDINESS Fully hardy
ZONE 3
HEIGHT 1.5–2.5m (5–8ft)
SPREAD 60cm (24in)
CULTIVATION Fertile, moist but well-drained soil. Full sun.

Aquilegia vulgaris 'William Guiness' I think columbines have more innate charm than almost any other flower; they are a must for my garden. Their initial contribution comes in the form of highly decorative foliage, with each leaf divided into individual rounded leaflets, which continue to look good once flowering is finished towards the end of May or early June. Columbines are found in a wide range of colours, but among the best are those with dark sultry tones. The deep maroon, nodding flowers of *Aquilegia vulgaris* 'William Guiness' deserve to be studied in detail: each intricately shaped bloom displays an inner cup edged in pale pinkish-white, with wing-like outer petals and distinctive spurs. The overall shape of the plant is satisfyingly elegant: straight, slender stems rise from the centre of a clump of pretty leaves and are topped with flowers that are lovely from a distance and exquisite in close-up. I cannot get enough of them and dot them throughout the border wherever there is a bit of dappled shade. Once the flowers have faded, I generally allow the seeds to ripen before chopping down the stems and giving them a good shake over gaps in the planting, where there is more than a fair chance that they will germinate. Columbines are promiscuous perennials, and if you do want to prevent them from self-seeding, cut the stems off as soon as the flowers have passed their best.

Aquilegia vulgaris
 'William Guiness'
COMMON NAME Columbine
HARDINESS Fully hardy
ZONE 5
HEIGHT 90cm (3ft)
SPREAD 45cm (18in)
CULTIVATION Fertile, moist
 but well-drained soil.
 Full sun to partial shade.

Papaver somniferum double black form

Few flowers evoke such a strong sense of enchantment as the opium poppy. Mankind may have been susceptible to the addictive powers of opium for centuries, but my craving is for the plant's sublimely beautiful and ephemeral flowers. The entire poppy is an asset to the garden: its tall stems and serrated foliage are tinged with a glaucous, blue-green hue and the developing buds hang their heads coyly until they are about to burst open.

When they do, the unfurling petals resemble crumpled tissue paper before they smooth out like the wings of an emerging butterfly. The flowers of both the single and double black forms combine the saturated colour of crushed mulberries with the texture of silk. In the double form, the petals are tightly crammed into each bud, before exploding into a voluptuous, ruffled flower. The single blooms are equally lovely – the sheen of the inner curve of each petal contrasting with a ring of pollen-tipped stamens.

After the petals fall, the rounded seedpods continue to add a decorative element to the garden. Unless these are later removed they will self-seed prolifically – producing progeny in a range of colours if they are allowed to cross breed. To ensure you get the colour you want, sow commercially produced seed where it is to flower. These hardy annuals produce some of the loveliest of all flowers: their fleeting charms may only last a few days, but the memory will continue to nourish you until next year.

Papaver somniferum double black form

COMMON NAME Opium poppy
HARDINESS Fully hardy
ZONE 7
HEIGHT 1.2m (4ft)
SPREAD 30cm (12in)
CULTIVATION Fertile, well-drained soil. Full sun.

Cosmos atrosanguineus If, like me, you find chocolate one of life's great pleasures, why not include it in your garden? *Cosmos atrosanguineus* earns its common name of chocolate cosmos on two counts: the colour of its flowers – which are a deep mahogany – and their delicious chocolatey aroma that assails our senses most powerfully on a warm, summer evening. The flowers which are borne on slender stems tinged with dark red, are daisy shaped with an outer ring of velvety petals arranged around a dark centre. They last from mid-summer to the first frosts, and regular deadheading will encourage further blooms. A basal clump of attractive dark green leaves provides a fitting backdrop.

I love to combine this exotic-looking perennial with the red-leaved grass *Imperata cylindrica* 'Rubra', adding a dash of California poppy, *Eschscholzia californica*, to brighten the mix. It should always be positioned close to the edge of the border, or grown in a container, where it will be within easy sniffing distance. *Cosmos atrosanguineus* is only borderline for hardiness and may be lost after a severe frost; so protect it with a generous layer of mulch before the worst of the winter weather sets in.

Cosmos atrosanguineus
COMMON NAME Chocolate cosmos
HARDINESS Frost hardy
ZONE 9
HEIGHT 75cm (30in)
SPREAD 45cm (18in)
CULTIVATION Moderately fertile, moist but well-drained soil. Full sun.

Dahlia 'Rip City' Not so long ago dahlias were thought old-fashioned and were relegated to the periphery of gardening. They featured strongly in the mostly male preserve of growing for showing and were often to be found in gaudy colours, keeping company with the garden gnome. However, I have always had a soft spot for dahlias, many of which are truly beautiful, and thought their potential was generally underrated. It seems I was not alone, for the dahlia is on the up and up, with a wealth of new varieties in wonderful shades. *Dahlia* 'Rip City' is a prime example: classified as a Medium Semi-cactus type dahlia, it has large flowers with curved and rolled petals in the most voluptuous deep claret, a richly saturated shade that drips with glamour.

Dahlias deserve to be respected as valuable garden plants; used judiciously they bring style and presence to a mixed planting scheme. Choose your variety carefully and position colours to complement the surrounding plants. The exotic flowers of 'Rip City' work well with bronze or plum foliage, and dusky flowered companions. Dahlias are not fully hardy and the tubers need to be lifted and stored over winter. They should be started off under cover in spring, and not planted out until all danger of frost is passed. If, as I do, you garden in a warm sheltered area, you can leave them in the ground throughout the year provided they are protected with a deep layer of mulch in the winter.

Dahlia 'Rip City'
HARDINESS Frost tender
ZONE 9
HEIGHT 1.2m (4ft)
SPREAD 60cm (24in)
CULTIVATION Fertile, humus-rich, well-drained soil. Full sun.
OTHER VARIETIES *Dahlia* 'Arabian night' – this Small Decorative type dahlia has luscious, dark maroon flowers. *D.* 'Moor Place' – a beautiful Pompon dahlia with small rounded heads of tightly packed petals in rich burgundy. *D.* 'Summer Night' – this produces large, deep crimson, Medium Cactus type flowers.

Salvia discolor

Although it is something of an oddity, and far from common in the garden, this perennial achieves an extraordinary blend of understated exoticism and warrants planting more often. I first spied it – and that is the perfect word, for it hardly stands out in a crowd – nestling at the base of a timber arch, in the ornamental vegetable garden at The Old Rectory in Farnborough, Oxfordshire. Small, inky black flowers were peeping out from elongated, pale green calyces – an effect created by a soft, woolly covering of tiny white hairs. The flowers appear in a vertical stack on the top of the branching stems in late summer and continue well into autumn: their unique colour combination of liquorice black and mint green is arresting, and always makes a good talking-point.

However, the subtle qualities of this plant can make it rather difficult to place in the garden, for it is all too easily lost among big, colourful companions. Find a spot where it will be seen on its own, with neither too light nor too dark a background – which will make either the calyces or the flowers disappear. A native of Peru, it benefits from a warm, sheltered position with plenty of sunshine. This is not a showy plant, but if you're looking for something a little different, I guarantee you will not be disappointed.

Salvia discolor
COMMON NAME Andean silver-leafed sage
HARDINESS Frost tender
ZONE 9
HEIGHT 45cm (18in)
SPREAD 30cm (12in)
CULTIVATION Moderately fertile, humus-rich, well-drained soil.
  Full sun.

Scabiosa atropurpurea 'Chile Black'

This striking biennial or short-lived perennial is an exotic version of the more familiar mauve or white forms of the pincushion flower. Pretty, toothed leaves form a clump at the base of the plant, above which slender, wiry stems hold aloft the flowers, wafting and bending in the slightest breeze. Each small flower opens from a nearly black bud and develops into a dome-shaped cluster of tiny, individual flowerheads. The colour is an intense aubergine that appears rather more crimson in strong sun and black as thunder in dull light. The surface of each inky flower is punctuated by minute stamens flecked with contrasting pale cream pollen – like little dabs of light on a dark, velvet cushion.

Flowering lasts throughout the summer and well into autumn, and regular dead-heading will encourage the production of further blooms – if you cut the stems while they are still at their peak you can also enjoy long-lasting cut flowers for the house. This plant makes an excellent contribution to the border, mixing well with bronze-leaved or dark-stemmed perennials, and providing a sharp contrast to orange or yellow flowers and acid green foliage. Ideally, grow it in a large group in order to maximise the impact of the dusky flowers; alternatively, intermingle it with neighbouring plants to add a bit of spice to the overall planting.

Scabiosa atropurpurea 'Chile Black'
COMMON NAME Sweet scabious/Pincushion flower
HARDINESS Fully hardy
ZONE 8
HEIGHT 60cm (24in)
SPREAD 23cm (9in)
CULTIVATION Moderately fertile, well-drained, preferably neutral to slightly alkaline soil. Full sun.

Iris 'Langport Wren'

When one is so spoilt for choice, selecting a favourite dark iris is as difficult as choosing a single chocolate from a box of the best Belgian truffles. However, this particular stunner has gained a firm following and for good reason. It is among the most reliable and free-flowering bearded irises in my garden, with gently undulating, rather than frilly, petals. Falling into the Intermediate Bearded category, the upper section of its branching stems is laden with flowers, with new blooms appearing as the first begin to fade. It is undoubtedly their colouring that makes them stand out from the crowd. Both the standards and the falls are an intensely rich burgundy, with even darker veining marking the petals and softly tactile, rust-brown beards in the throat of each fall.

The flowers are accompanied by upright, blade-like leaves that continue to make a structural contribution to the border long after the flowers have faded. When you snap off the spent flower-heads, the petals ooze a deep purple liquid that temporarily stains your hand like blackberry juice. Make sure you plant shallowly: the knobbly rhizome benefits from being baked by the sun and should just be visible above the surface of the soil. Criticism that iris flowers are too fleeting to make them worth growing holds no sway with me; I'd happily wait all year for just two weeks of such beauty.

Iris 'Langport Wren'

HARDINESS Fully hardy
ZONE 4
HEIGHT 65cm (26in)
SPREAD 40cm (16in)
CULTIVATION Fertile, humus-rich, well-drained soil. Full sun.
OTHER VARIETIES *Iris chrysographes*–this slender species iris has incredibly elegant flowers as near to true black as you will find. *I.* 'George'–the imperial purple flowers of this Reticulata iris are only 12cm (4¾in) tall and make a welcome appearance as winter gives way to spring. *I.* 'Pumpin' Iron'–dramatic, black cherry colouring packs a punch in this diminutive, early-flowering iris. *I.* 'Superstition'–voluptuous, purple-black flowers with a delicious scent, top sturdy 90cm (3ft) tall stems.

Viola 'Bowles' Black' The petite flowers of the viola are always enchanting – their smiling 'faces' delighted me as a child and have found a place in my garden ever since. They come in an ever-increasing array of colours, but among the most captivating are those with nearly black flowers. *Viola* 'Bowles Black' is an excellent example with inky black, velvet-textured petals heightened by a glowing, golden centre. The flowers are small and hover in abundance over a low mat of green foliage. The clump will gradually widen but retains its attractive, compact habit.

These diminutive perennials are invaluable in the garden, filling gaps at the front of a border, dotted among alpines in a raised bed and peeking demurely over the top of a pot. They will flower on and off throughout the season from spring to autumn – regular deadheading will encourage a new flush of flowers. Individual clumps not only spread but frequently self-seed and you will find their kitten faces peeping up at you from the most unlikely places. All violas bring charm to the garden and when this is coupled with colouring as intense and black as thunder, the effect is slightly unsettling, yet absolutely irresistible.

Viola 'Bowles' Black'
HARDINESS Fully hardy
ZONE 4
HEIGHT 10cm (4in)
SPREAD 20cm (8in)
CULTIVATION Fertile, humus-rich, moist but well-drained soil. Sun to partial shade.
OTHER VARIETIES *Viola* 'Molly Sanderson' – spreads slowly to form a neat clump of matt black flowers with a yellow eye. *V.* 'Roscastle Black' – large quantities of almost black flowers which smother the leaves.

Tulipa 'Queen of Night'

I adore tulips, looking forward with anticipation to their appearance each spring, but if I had to choose just one, this would be it. There are few flowers that can match its quality and exoticism. Beautiful in form, it bears perfectly proportioned, upright, goblet-shaped flowers that open voluptuously during daylight and close again at dusk. The petals have a silky sheen that gleams in the sunshine, making it hard to resist stroking the flowers. The intensity of their deep claret colour is hard to define: it's certainly the closest shade to black in a tulip and in low evening light it appears sexily sombre.

Tulipa 'Queen of Night' will grow successfully in the border, but deep planting – at least 10cm (4in) and 15cm (6in) would be even better – is essential to encourage flowering in subsequent years. As with all tulips, deadhead when the flowers have faded, but don't be tempted to cut off the leaves until they have died down, in order for their goodness to be returned to the bulb. My preferred way to grow them is in a really generous container, where they look stunning on their own or in combination with other tulips in contrasting colours. *T.* 'Shirley' is a good choice, the purple-flecked edges of its pure white petals picking up on the deeper colour of its companion. For a more daring partnership, try *T.* 'Prinses Irene', a dazzling orange variety with purple streaks on the outer petals.

Tulipa 'Queen of Night'

HARDINESS Fully hardy
ZONE 4
HEIGHT 60cm (24in)
SPREAD 15cm (6in)
CULTIVATION Fertile, moist but well-drained soil. Full sun.
OTHER VARIETIES *Tulipa* 'Black Parrot' – its showy blooms with blowsy, feathered petals are deepest burgundy *T.* 'Black Swan' – well-shaped, silky-textured, purple flowers are held on sturdy stems. *T.* 'Arabian Mystery' – violet-purple flowers with creamy centres and a silvery-white edge. *T.* 'Astarte' – its glistening, plum-coloured flowers are edged with a sliver of palest lilac.

climbers for a shady wall

If, like me, you have an urban garden surrounded on all sides by high walls and towering buildings, you will know what it is to deal with shady boundaries. Suburban and rural gardens are also likely to have at least one shaded area; at the risk of stating the obvious, for every south-facing wall or fence there is a north-facing one on the other side. I have come to terms with even the darkest corners of my own garden, revelling in the beautiful climbers that adorn its elegant brick walls.

There are several things you can do to make the most of the available light and improve the chances of success for borderline plants. Painting the flat surfaces with a pale, light-reflective colour, such as cream, dove grey or off-white, will considerably increase the amount of light by bouncing it off the walls or fences. Mirrors are both popular as design elements and useful for reflecting light; positioned behind trellis, they maximise the brightness of the dimmest corner. In this way a sunken basement or narrow passageway can become a hospitable home for shade-loving climbers.

However, there is no miracle that will make your shady spot bright enough to accommodate true sun-lovers; if you insist on planting the right plant in the wrong place you will merely be setting yourself up to fail. It is far better to accept the limitations of the site and choose from a range of climbers that happily tolerate a sunless wall. And what a choice – many of the loveliest of all climbers fall within this remit and would be included among my favourites regardless of their preference for shade.

There are many different types of shade, from the deep, dank shade created by tall, enclosing walls and buildings to the full but unoppressive shade of a north-facing wall or fence in a generally open setting. Semi-shaded areas have sun for at least a couple of hours every day, and the light, dappled shade found at the edge of the canopy of a deciduous tree is perhaps the easiest to deal with. In this chapter you will find suitable climbers for all these sites.

When growing climbers, I have occasionally tried to push the boundaries by selecting plants that are less frequently suggested for shade – often with favourable results. In particular, many roses and clematis prove very successful, yet most books recommend only the same small handful of varieties for shade. I include some alternatives that fare equally well and deserve to be more widely grown as shade-tolerant plants.

Many suitable climbers share a restrained palette of flower colours, with white, cream and pastel shades dominating the scene. This is no bad thing, for pale tones are more easily seen in low light, glowing sublimely in the shadows. Decorative leaves are as valuable as flowers in a plant that is destined to clothe a wall for any length of time. The flowers will fade, but evergreen foliage looks good throughout the year. Whatever you choose will ultimately enhance the shady vertical spaces in your garden.

Clematis 'Miss Bateman'

Several varieties of clematis are regularly recommended for shady walls, but I was certain the range of large-flowered cultivars could be expanded, so I have been experimenting with different types on my own north-facing wall – which never receives direct sun – with encouraging results. *Clematis* 'Miss Bateman' has proved one of the most successful: it is currently happily flowering through its fifth season, producing an abundance of flowers across the plant despite the lack of sun. The disc-like single flowers are breathtaking in their simplicity, their milky-white petals providing a clean backdrop for the burgundy-tipped anthers at the centre of each bloom. Another asset is its compact growth, which makes it perfect for a wide variety of uses and situations.

This is a group 2 clematis, so it bears flowers in early to mid-season (late spring to early summer), on side-shoots that emerge from growth produced during the previous year, and it occasionally flowers again at the end of the summer on the current year's growth. When it comes to pruning, all that is required is to trim each stem to a pair of strong, visible buds in early spring – try varying the height of the cuts to encourage an even spread of flowers. To encourage a second flush of blooms, I deadhead the early flowers as soon as they have faded. Late season seed-heads may be left in place, where their fluffy rings of stamens will add a decorative element through the autumn.

Clematis 'Miss Bateman'

HARDINESS Fully hardy
ZONE 5
HEIGHT 2.5m (8ft)
CULTIVATION Fertile, humus-rich, moist but well-drained soil. Sun to partial shade.
OTHER VARIETIES *Clematis* 'Mrs Cholmondeley' – large, mauve flowers and chocolate brown anthers. *C.* 'Lasurstern' – show-stopping, large-flowered cultivar with rich blue-purple flowers – copes admirably with shade. *C.* 'Nelly Moser' – an old favourite, with large, pink-mauve flowers, each petal with a deeper central band.

Hedera helix 'Glacier'

Hedera helix 'Glacier' If asked to name a good climber for shade, most of us would immediately think of ivy. Easy to dismiss as dull and predictable, ivies are unbeatable shade-tolerant plants – one of the few that thrive in deep shade – with an endless range of leaf size, texture and colour. *Hedera helix* 'Glacier' is a cultivar of our native ivy and has small, grey-green, triple-lobed leaves, each one uniquely patterned with pale grey and cream variegation. The overall effect is cool and icy, the silver tones creating endless permutations across the leaves.

Many variegated ivies tend to lose the best of their colouring in deep shade, with the yellow cultivars being most susceptible, but I find that 'Glacier' retains its variegation particularly well and brightens even the darkest corner. Ivy is an exceptionally versatile plant and shouldn't be confined to walls and fences. This variety looks equally wonderful trailing over the sides of a large pot or window-box, and its stems can be allowed to wend along the garden floor, providing valuable ground cover beneath a canopy of trees. 'Glacier' is one of the more compact varieties, but if it starts to outgrow its allotted space you can cut it back; it will quickly refurnish itself and look better than ever.

Hedera helix 'Glacier'

COMMON NAME Ivy

HARDINESS Fully hardy

ZONE 6

HEIGHT 2m (6½ft)

CULTIVATION Fertile, humus-rich, moist but well-drained soil. Sun or shade.

OTHER VARIETIES *H. helix* 'Oro di Bogliasco' – the medium-sized leaves have golden yellow centres edged in emerald green and retain their variegation well in shade. *H. helix* 'Green Ripple' – a beautifully shaped ivy with large, sharply jagged, dark green leaves. *H. helix* 'Pedata' – the shape of each grey-green leaf is perfectly described by its common name, bird's-foot ivy.

Hydrangea anomala subsp. petiolaris

I am becoming increasingly fond of hydrangeas, and being able to grow this one vertically, while at the same time clothing a shady wall, gives me the perfect excuse to include another example in my garden. This woody climber is deciduous and its twisting, bronze stems are completely naked in winter. Attractive, dark green, rounded leaves smother the plant in spring and summer, before turning gold in autumn. They are accompanied in midsummer by flattened heads of white flowers, whose inner buds are tightly shut, while the outer ones open wide to display four or five snowy petals. This is a climber with subtle charms that becomes exceedingly pretty when in flower and can cope with quite deep shade.

Give your newly planted climbing hydrangea a good start by tying young stems to the wall – at this stage you can control the way they cover the surface. Once it takes off, the self-clinging aerial roots will take over the job of hanging onto the wall. Although it must have taken many years to do so, I have seen this climber completely clothing the side of a two-storey building. However, if you are looking for something a little smaller don't despair, as it can be pruned hard in spring to keep it compact and is therefore eminently suitable for the small garden.

Hydrangea anomala subsp. *petiolaris*
COMMON NAME Climbing hydrangea
HARDINESS Fully hardy
ZONE 4
HEIGHT 15m (50ft)
CULTIVATION Moderately fertile, humus-rich, moist but well-drained soil. Sun or shade.

Lonicera japonica 'Halliana' Honeysuckle is so evocative of a midsummer garden that it earns its place among the best loved climbers. Although it is frequently grown in full sun, many forms will thrive in a reasonable degree of shade. The plant climbs by twining its stems around any available support, and can grow at an alarming rate. The distinctive tubular flowers of this vigorous cultivar are creamy white when they first appear, ageing to golden yellow. The flowers are not only pretty: they are also extremely sweetly scented and their fragrance carries on the warm air of a summer evening. Create classic, romantic combinations with climbing roses and clematis and you will have difficulty tearing yourself away.

With a scrambling habit, honeysuckle could never be described as neat or compact; it prefers to be allowed to sprawl over an arch or into the lower branches of a small tree. By all means grow it on a wall or fence, but expect the long whippy stems to give it a charming, if unkempt, lived-in look by the end of the season. To prevent it from becoming too unwieldy, prune out a couple of the older stems entirely and give the rest of the plant a hard clipping with shears in spring; tying the new stems to supports on the wall will help to maintain a manageable framework.

Lonicera japonica
'Halliana'
COMMON NAME Japanese
  honeysuckle
HARDINESS Fully hardy
ZONE 4
HEIGHT 10m (33ft)
CULTIVATION Fertile, humus-
  rich, moist but well-
  drained soil. Full sun
  to partial shade.

Parthenocissus henryana
When it comes to smothering a substantial area of wall or fence, foliage takes precedence; an attractive leaf can have far more long-term appeal than an ephemeral flush of flowers. Few climbers can match the Chinese Virginia creeper for decorative foliage; although it is less well known than its relatives, the Boston ivy and the Virginia creeper, *Parthenocissus henryana* is arguably the loveliest of the lot. It has three- or five-lobed, dark green leaves, each one picked out in white along its veins; the satisfying shape and contrasting colouring make for an eye-catching combination.

As a bonus, the foliage turns brilliant shades of orange and scarlet in the autumn before it falls, but therein lies the rub: in an ideal world it would miraculously become evergreen, regaining its spring hues the following year. Despite its lack of winter foliage, this is still an exceptionally good climber and deserves to be more widely grown. It is tolerant of light to full shade, although its autumn colour will be best in partial shade, and it has a neat habit – clinging tightly to the wall by means of tiny suckers – with each leaf slightly overlapping the next. However, it is definitely a climber for a large space: trying to restrict its growth to fit a small space will be a constant battle.

Parthenocissus henryana
COMMON NAME Chinese Virginia creeper
HARDINESS Frost hardy
ZONE 7
HEIGHT 10m (30ft)
CULTIVATION Fertile, moist but well-drained soil. Sun or shade.

Pileostegia viburnoides Although it belongs to the same family as the climbing hydrangea, this lovely climber is less well known than its relative, despite having the added bonus of evergreen leaves. These are both elegant and unusual: long and slender in shape with dark green colouring and a leathery texture. They provide dense coverage on a large wall and are an attractive backdrop to the flowers, which appear in late summer and last well into autumn – a time when few other climbers are in flower. They consist of tiny, individual, star-shaped blooms, which combine to form large, frothy panicles. Their pale creamy colour helps them to stand out in a shady spot.

In the wild, this climber attaches itself to trees and cliffs, but in the garden it is best suited to growing on a north-facing wall where its aerial roots can gain a firm foothold, although it will also sprawl happily over a tree stump. Growth is slow and steady, but eventually it becomes a handsome and impressive specimen. A light trim can be done at any time to keep it within bounds, but any more substantial pruning should be carried out in spring. This is a stylish climber with many assets, not least its trouble-free reputation and tolerance of a wide range of situations and growing conditions: it always surprises me that it is not grown more often.

Pileostegia
viburnoides
HARDINESS Fully hardy
  (borderline)
ZONE 7
HEIGHT 6m (20ft)
CULTIVATION Fertile, moist
  but well-drained soil.
  Sun or shade.

Rosa 'Madame Alfred Carrière' First introduced in 1879, this long-established favourite has stood the test of time, thanks to a combination of strong growth and gentle good looks. Its somewhat unstructured flowers have softly textured, milky-white petals enhanced with a hint of pale shell pink. Their wonderfully unkempt, old-rose appearance and tea-rose fragrance give them a charm that is hard to match. However, their lack of stiffness means that a heavy downpour can leave them looking extremely dishevelled. The plentiful foliage is light green and there are few thorns on the strong, upright stems.

The first small buds open in the early part of May and quickly cover the plant, particularly on a lightly shaded wall. Single blooms continue to be produced on and off throughout the summer, with a more substantial second flowering in September – regular deadheading will help to encourage further flowers. Growth is vigorous and long, whippy stems appear with alarming speed. Tie these in as near to horizontal as possible before they get too unwieldy and catch you in the eye. Bending the long stems encourages new flowering shoots to break along their length; if you allow the stems to remain vertical, flowers will be produced only at the very top of the plant where they cannot easily be seen.

Rosa 'Madame Alfred Carrière'
HARDINESS Fully hardy
ZONE 6
HEIGHT 5m (16ft)
CULTIVATION Moderately fertile, humus-rich, moist but well-drained soil. Sun to partial shade.
OTHER VARIETIES *Rosa* 'Albéric Barbier' – Rambler with delicately scented, cream flowers. *R.* 'Maigold' – climber with abundant semi-double, deep golden flowers. *R.* 'New Dawn' – a vigorous climber with fragrant, blush pink flowers.

Schizophragma integrifolium

This deciduous climber is yet another member of the shade-loving hydrangea family and is understandably easy to confuse with the climbing form, *Hydrangea anomala* subsp. *petiolaris* (see page 98). However, if you are looking for something equally lovely, but a little more unusual, this is the one to choose. The elegantly arching leaves are slightly pointed toward their tips and are accompanied by startling sprays of creamy white flowers in midsummer. These are composed of clusters of tiny, individual flowers and tear-shaped, flattened bracts that dance in the breeze like feathers on an Ascot hat.

Attaching itself to its support by means of aerial roots, this climber is happiest on a wall, but will also clamber up a large tree, sprawl over a tree stump or smother a strongly constructed fence. Its stems will benefit from tying in firmly when first planted, until they are able to gain a firm foothold. Pruning should be confined to the dormant season, when any surplus long, clingy growth may be removed, but avoid taking off the shorter, lateral branches on which the flowering buds will later be formed. In the right spot this can be a spectacular climber: give it shade – even full shade will do – and plenty of space, and watch the flowers glow in the shadows.

Schizophragma integrifolium
HARDINESS Fully hardy
ZONE 6
HEIGHT 12m (40ft)
CULTIVATION Moderately fertile, humus-rich, moist but well-drained soil. Sun to partial shade.

decorative herbs

In recent years there has been a significant resurgence in the popularity of medicinal and culinary herbs, and with it a new appreciation of their decorative qualities. Quite apart from their obvious usefulness, many herbs are extremely pretty. They range in habit from ground-hugging thymes to statuesque columns of bay. Foliage can be every shape from thin and grass-like to large and glossy, and colours vary from pale silver-grey to bronze, purple and rich, dark green, occasionally striped or mottled with cream or gold variegation.

Herbs are garden-worthy in their own right: some of the most successful show gardens at prestigious gardening events – such as the Chelsea, Hampton Court Palace and Tatton Park Flower Shows – are packed with herbs. They may be given their own, dedicated area within the garden where they make incredibly pretty combinations of flower and foliage within woven willow compartments or galvanized metal containers. Others are mixed into the main planting scheme; this is particularly evident with the new, more naturalistic style of planting, which incorporates wildflowers as well as herbs in the mix.

Break the rules when choosing where to grow herbs at home. Why confine them to the kitchen garden or a couple of dull pots by the back door when you can let them infiltrate the main ornamental flower-beds, pop them into a hanging basket or intermingle them with petunias in a window-box? Herbs thrive in containers: they look charming tumbling out of an old watering can or a battered enamel bucket, while traditional materials such as lead, stone and terracotta all make attractive backdrops. Alternatively, aim for a more contemporary effect, with mirrored, stainless-steel or lead planters.

Of course herbs have always been part of the main body of the garden. Lavender and rosemary are as common in the rose garden as they are among fellow herbs. They provide year-round structure and give shape to the winter garden, as well as scent and flowers in summer. Now is the time to widen the repertoire to include less obvious herbs in unexpected places. Curly-leaved parsley makes a wonderfully vibrant, emerald green edging to a herbaceous border, while the lacy foliage of bronze fennel looks perfectly at home among perennials and grasses. Try designing a modern version of the traditional, knot garden, updating the formal shapes with an asymmetric format.

Quite apart from the visual pleasure that herbs bring to the garden is their significant contribution to the other senses: it's impossible not to brush a hand through their aromatic foliage, bend down to smell a flower or pick a leaf to chew. While herbs are undeniably important for flavouring food, producing infusions and – in the hands of practised experts – concocting natural medicinal remedies, it's equally valid to appreciate them for their sheer beauty as plants. The answer is to grow enough to allow some to be picked, while the rest add another layer of beauty to the garden.

Allium schoenoprasum Chives are instantly recognisable as members of the onion family. They are reliably perennial, spreading to form a large clump of tiny bulbs that may be lifted and divided every few years to develop new colonies. Long, thin, cylindrical leaves appear in spring, followed by pinky mauve, globe-like flowers that open from little drumstick buds.

If you are growing chives primarily for culinary use, it is best to remove the flower stems before flowering in order to encourage further leaf production. However, I love the effect of their mass of flowers and cannot bring myself to cut them off. Nevertheless, I do manage to harvest sufficient leaves to garnish salads and soups by cutting small sections of the clump right back to within 4cm (1½in) of ground level. This can be done several times during the season and new foliage soon takes its place.

Try growing chives as a decorative edging to an ornamental bed, or use the spiky foliage to provide a valuable visual punctuation mark in a mixed herb planting. They thrive quite happily in a pot provided they get plenty of water, a bit of shade and an occasional boost with some liquid feed. Legend has it that planting chives next to roses will help to prevent black spot in the latter; it hasn't quite done the trick with mine, but perhaps you'll have better luck.

Allium schoenoprasum

COMMON NAME Chives
HARDINESS Fully hardy
ZONE 4
HEIGHT 12–25cm (5–10in)
SPREAD 5–10cm (2–4in)
CULTIVATION Fertile, moist but well-drained soil. Full sun to partial shade.

Foeniculum vulgare 'Purpureum'

Bronze fennel is among the most beautiful of all herbs for general garden use. It sends up tall, elegant stems each spring and by the first week of May they are already looking good in my London garden. Soft, feathery, dull bronze foliage adorns the plant; it appears along the length of each stem, but is most lovely where it billows out towards the top. Throughout midsummer the light, frothy foliage is resplendent and tiny water droplets cling to the airy network of stems after rain. The aromatic, aniseed-flavoured leaves can be added to salads and are often used as a garnish for fish dishes.

This perennial herb is invaluable in the mixed border – although plants are best replaced every three to four years with vigorous new stock. It provides an excellent foil to stiff-leaved neighbours and softens the effect of solid, rounded flowers such as dahlias. I use it as an alternative to tall grasses: it adds the same movement and informality while remaining upright in shape and compact in spread. By mid-July flowering is well under way. The flattened heads of tiny, individual flowers in mustard-yellow are pretty enough, but are not the dominant reason for growing a plant with such exquisite, filigree foliage. Choose the straightforward *Foeniculum vulgare* if you prefer paler, fresh green leaves with the same airy softness, but bear in mind that bronze fennel is slightly hardier than this species and will have a better chance of coming through a cold, wet winter.

Foeniculum vulgare 'Purpureum'
COMMON NAME Bronze fennel
HARDINESS Fully hardy
ZONE 4
HEIGHT 1.8m (6ft)
SPREAD 45cm (18in)
CULTIVATION Fertile, well-drained soil. Full sun.

Laurus nobilis Few herbs can be said to provide a substantial year-round contribution to the garden, but bay is one such. The large, pointed, evergreen leaves are fresh and bright when young, maturing to a darker green, and are familiar to most of us as the dried, tan-coloured, whole leaves used in soups and stews, often as part of a bouquet garni. In the garden, they provide a backdrop for tiny, creamy yellow flowers, which nestle among the foliage in spring, followed in the autumn by almost black berries.

Bay is wonderfully accommodating in its readiness to be clipped and shaped. I grow several as large standards – rounded, lollipop heads on top of straight, clear stems – and another as a cone. These add valuable height to the herb garden, their blocks of dense foliage acting as solid full stops amid a froth of informality, and work beautifully in pots. Give plants a trim in spring to maintain the required shape and encourage a flush of new leaves.

Bay is a native of the Mediterranean and is redolent of gardens beneath endless blue skies. It proves hardy in all but the least hospitable sites, but can be scorched by exposure to cold winds. For peace of mind, choose a sunny, sheltered spot.

Laurus nobilis
COMMON NAME Bay laurel
HARDINESS Frost hardy to fully hardy
ZONE 7
HEIGHT 12m (40ft)
SPREAD 10m (33ft)
CULTIVATION Fertile, moist but well-drained soil. Full sun to partial shade.

Mentha suaveolens 'Variegata' There are
so many delicious and good-looking mints that
you will probably choose to grow more than one.
Most are rampant growers in the open garden and
behave like thugs in a mixed planter containing a
range of other herbs. The trick is to give them their
own container, or to plant them in a plastic pot and
sink it directly into the ground where neighbouring
plants will disguise the rim – the confined space
will restrain the roots and keep the plant compact.

By contrast, the lovely pineapple mint,
Mentha suaveolens 'Variegata', is reasonably
well behaved and may be allowed to associate
with other plants. It produces pretty green leaves
with creamy variegation and a softly hairy texture.
The colouring will brighten a mixed herb bed, the
front of a sunny herbaceous border or a hanging
basket. Regular picking will encourage a compact,
bushy habit and the leaves can be used as a
garnish. This mint is perhaps rather more
decorative than culinary; I suggest you grow at
least two or three different types to give you the
best of all worlds. If, like me, you're partial to a cup
of mint tea, once you've tasted the real thing made
from freshly picked leaves, you'll never again settle
for a packet of dried tea.

Mentha suaveolens 'Variegata'
COMMON NAME Pineapple mint
HARDINESS Fully hardy
ZONE 6
HEIGHT 40–60cm (16–24in)
SPREAD indefinite
CULTIVATION Moderately fertile, moist but well-drained soil.
  Full sun.
OTHER VARIETIES _Mentha_ x _piperita_ f. _citrata_ – Eau de Cologne
  mint has attractive purple-edged foliage. Tie some leaves
  together in a small bunch and hang it under the running tap for
  an aromatic bath. _M. spicata_ – spearmint is the most popular
  culinary mint, widely grown and suitable for a multitude of
  dishes. _M._ x _gracilis_ 'Variegata' – ginger mint is highly
  decorative, with variegated, green and golden yellow foliage.

Tanacetum parthenium 'Aureum'

Tanacetum parthenium 'Aureum' I frequently sing the praises of plants with yellow-green foliage and applaud the contribution they make to the appearance of the garden: this is equally true of herbs. Golden feverfew fits the bill perfectly; its leaves have an attractive, intricate shape and vivid, acid-green colouring. In early summer clusters of daisy-like, white flowers with golden centres smother the plant completely; these may be removed if you feel they detract from the foliage, but I prefer to enjoy them for a couple of weeks. The plant has a compact habit, which can be maintained by cutting back the foliage and flowered stems to encourage a new flush of leaves. Do this as the flowers begin to fade if you want to stop it self-seeding.

This herb was generally prized for its medicinal rather than culinary properties and is now largely grown for its decorative qualities alone. I have seen it saving many planting combinations from banality; the vibrancy of its foliage sings like a clear, high note among a sea of dull, mid-green tones. It provides a welcome contrast in a mixed herb container or window-box and it looks equally good at the front of an ornamental border or raised bed, where the colour will retain its vivacity throughout the season. Although fully hardy, this short-lived perennial will need to be replaced regularly.

Tanacetum parthenium 'Aureum'
COMMON NAME Golden feverfew
HARDINESS Fully hardy
ZONE 6
HEIGHT 45–60cm (18–24in)
SPREAD 30cm (12in)
CULTIVATION Well-drained soil. Full sun.

Salvia officinalis 'Purpurascens'

Salvia officinalis 'Purpurascens' This evergreen perennial is a member of the vast sage family. Native to the Mediterranean region, it forms a shrubby mound of branching stems with textured foliage in shades of dusky purple, green and grey. The leaves are elongated and have a dry surface that reminds me of a cat's tongue. I am particularly drawn to the subtle range of colouring to be found within a single clump, with the new leaves having the strongest purple tone. This is a herb to plant in large groups if you have the space; it combines well with the pink, mauve or blue flowers that adorn many other herbs, including chives, thyme and lavender, and it contrasts beautifully with plain green or silver foliage. Use it to fill the spaces between low box hedges in a parterre or grow it in a container with other herbs or ornamental plants.

Purple sage is hardy and will come through the winter successfully, provided it doesn't sit in waterlogged soil for any length of time – growing it through gravel will help to minimise wet, winter conditions. To keep the plant looking good and prevent it from becoming woody towards the base, give it a trim in spring, which will encourage the development of new leaves. This will mean sacrificing the lavender, summer flowers, but I think on balance that the foliage has greater appeal. After about five years, plants will inevitably deteriorate and should be replaced.

Salvia officinalis 'Purpurascens'
COMMON NAME Purple sage
HARDINESS Fully hardy
ZONE 6
HEIGHT 80cm (32in)
SPREAD 1m (3ft)
CULTIVATION Moderately fertile, humus-rich, moist but well-drained soil. Full sun.

Rosmarinus officinalis 'Miss Jessop's Upright' The distinctive aroma of rosemary is among my absolute favourites. Rubbing a few leaves between your fingers releases the full intensity of the essential oils and delivers a blast of invigorating perfume; a couple of sprigs enlivens the dullest dish. The evergreen foliage with its blue-grey colour has narrow leaves; nature's way of minimising water loss. In early to mid-spring the stems are covered in a sprinkling of small, but very pretty, pale blue flowers, which may occasionally appear again later in the year. This particular variety has strongly upright growth, with vertical stems pointing skyward. It is ideally suited to providing informal hedging and may be trimmed in spring after flowering has finished.

I have seen rosemary growing wild among the scrub-like vegetation of southern Provence, where plants cling to a thin layer of soil on the rocky hillsides. If you can recreate these conditions in the garden – with a position in full sun and well-drained soil – the rosemary will thrive. Containers also make a good home, and rosemary can withstand a bit of thirst should you occasionally forget to water them. Older plants tend to become bare and straggly near the base. They can be cut back hard in spring, but a youthful replacement may ultimately prove the better option.

Rosmarinus officinalis
  'Miss Jessop's
  Upright'
COMMON NAME Rosemary
HARDINESS Fully hardy
ZONE 8
HEIGHT 2m (6½ft)
SPREAD 1.2m (4ft)
CULTIVATION Moderately
  fertile, well-drained soil.
  Full sun.

Thymus 'Doone Valley' There is a seemingly
endless range from which to choose – some of
them ground-hugging, others becoming a shrubby
mound. *Thymus* 'Doone Valley' is among the most
ornamental; it forms a low-growing, rounded mat of
small, dark green leaves that are vividly marked with
a golden yellow variegation. This is spread irregularly
across the plant, so that some areas are solid green,
while others are generously splashed with gold.
In summer the evergreen foliage is almost entirely
obscured by a host of tiny, pinky mauve flowers.

Thymes can be dotted among other herbs
at the front edge of a border and be allowed to
sprawl onto the path, but they look equally
beautiful when given their own area. A complete
bed filled with an assortment of different thymes,
with their contrasting foliage and flower colours,
slowly evolves into a series of undulating, aromatic
hummocks, attracting a horde of butterflies and
bees. Thymes are also invaluable for raised beds
and containers and will fill crevices between paving
stones: try planting them en masse to form a
thyme pavement. Although thyme will cope with a
limited amount of wear and tear, it cannot survive
regular heavy traffic so ensure your pavement has
sufficient areas of stone, brick or gravel to act as
stepping stones between the thymes.

Thymus 'Doone Valley'

COMMON NAME Thyme
HARDINESS Fully hardy
ZONE 6
HEIGHT 12cm (5in)
SPREAD 35cm (14in)
CULTIVATION Well-drained, preferably neutral to alkaline soil.
  Full sun.
OTHER VARIETIES *Thymus pulegioides* 'Aureus' — golden lemon
  thyme with bright, yellow-green foliage and pale, lilac-pink
  flowers. *T. vulgaris* 'Silver Posie' — slightly taller variety whose
  variegated, green and cream foliage provides a silvery backdrop
  for mauve-pink flowers. *T. serpyllum* 'Pink Chintz' — low-growing
  thyme with softly hairy, grey-green leaves and pale pink flowers.

annuals and biennials

I came rather late to the glories of annuals and biennials, preferring to stick to the shrubs and perennials that could cope with the vagaries of the British climate year in year out. However, I have become increasingly drawn to the colour, glamour and incredible flowering capabilities of these lovely plants. Annuals are often associated with gaudy bedding schemes, so the range of elegant plants in subtle colours may come as a surprise. Grow them in large drifts of single varieties for maximum impact or dot them among other annuals or perennial grasses for an informal effect.

Of course, many of the plants that we grow as annuals are perennials in their native habitat. It is only when they are subjected to temperatures a couple of degrees below freezing that they turn up their toes. True annuals complete an entire life cycle in a year. Hardy annuals can withstand frost and their seed can be sown where they are to flower, producing roots and foliage before they get into real growth in the spring. They then flower, produce seed and shed it, before dying as the next generation germinates in the soil. Half-hardy annuals need protection from frost and should be started off under cover.

Biennials take two years to do the same thing, producing only roots and foliage in the first summer, and flowering and setting seed in the second. This sounds like a long time to wait, but once you get started you can sow in consecutive years to stagger the flowering, so that at least one group of biennials is in flower in any year.

Annuals make perfect filler plants: they can quickly smother an empty space with a block of summer-long colour or bridge gaps in a border while more permanent shrubs and perennials grow to fill their allotted space. They are also extremely useful in a newly acquired garden: while you make long-term decisions about placing trees and reshaping the lawn, they can be used to create an attractive-looking garden in the meantime.

If you have room, why not set aside an area as a cutting garden? Fill it with a range of colourful annuals and biennials and enjoy cut flowers for the house throughout the summer and well into autumn. Cutting will spur the plants into producing further flushes of flower and if you add bulbs as well you can extend the season still further. Sowing or planting in rows will make weeding and cutting easier and by leaving gaps between each line you will be able to reach the stems of every plant.

Growing plants from seed is incredibly satisfying: you start off with a few little packets and with some tender loving care and patience you can produce dozens of small plants that make a big impact in the garden. This is the perfect way to introduce children to gardening: once they see what they can achieve you will have sown the precious seed of a life-long fascination for plants.

Cerinthe major 'Purpurascens' I first saw this extraordinary hardy annual in a container at Great Dixter in East Sussex and was determined to have it growing in my garden the following year. Although it is easily raised from seed by sowing in pots in autumn and overwintering in a cold frame or by sowing in situ in late spring, I took a short cut when I spotted some young plants for sale at Merriments Nursery in East Sussex. That summer, the resulting display flowered over a long period and drew more admiring comments than any other plant in the garden. I continue to be fixated by its strangely alien beauty.

I think the appeal lies in its perfect combination of foliage and flowers, both in form and colour. Small, oval, blue-green leaves rise up the length of the stems, whose tips arch over coyly. The uppermost bracts are shaded with an intense glaucous blue and overlap one another as they cradle the small, tubular flowers. These pendulous blooms are a beautiful clear purple, and the overall effect created by the blend of colours is extremely arresting. As the flowers fade, they leave behind large black seeds that can either be collected or allowed to self-seed where they fall. A bell cloche will protect the young seedlings from the worst of the winter cold and wet.

Cerinthe major
 'Purpurascens'
COMMON NAME Honeywort
HARDINESS Fully hardy
ZONE 7
HEIGHT 60cm (2ft)
SPREAD 30cm (12in)
CULTIVATION Moderately
 fertile, moist but well-
 drained soil. Full sun.

Cosmos bipinnatus 'Purity'

I love the simple beauty of plants with daisy-shaped flowers and this is one of the best. The foliage is exceptionally light and pretty, with finely divided, lacy leaves that create a frothy effect when seen from a distance. When in full bloom, masses of snowy white flowers smother the plant, each one made up of a ring of pure white petals with a serrated edge around a central button of sunny yellow stamens. They have a freshness that cannot fail to make you feel happy and appear in abundance on tall stems throughout the summer and early autumn; regular deadheading will ensure the flowers keep coming.

White flowers enliven a dreary corner and glow in the evening light, while an entirely white planting scheme brings elegance to any garden. Alternatively, combine this easy-going annual with colourful neighbours: there are few plants it cannot be partnered with. Either way, be generous and plant enough to cut for the house, where the blooms can last for up to a fortnight in a vase. Use it to fill gaps between shrubs and dot it among perennials. I've also seen it used most effectively to fill a narrow border running along the entire length of a sunny house wall – clearly a case of the more the merrier.

Cosmos bipinnatus 'Purity'

COMMON NAME Cosmea
HARDINESS Half hardy
ZONE 9
HEIGHT 1.2m (4ft)
SPREAD 45cm (18in)
CULTIVATION Moderately fertile, moist but well-drained soil. Full sun.
OTHER VARIETIES *Cosmos bipinnatus* 'Daydream' – white outer petals are shaded deep pink towards the centre of the flower. Fully or semi-double feathery flowers in snowy white. *C. bipinnatus* 'Sonata White' – a more compact, pure white, single form that is perfect for the smaller garden.

Lathyrus odoratus 'Matucana'

Whenever I visit one of the major gardening shows, among the first places I head for are the floral marquees to see the sweet pea displays. There I can compare some established favourites with the new introductions, get a lungful of scent and buy some seed. There are many lovely varieties, but I've yet to see anything that surpasses this old garden stalwart. The flowers, which are smaller and simpler in shape than some of the more frilly newcomers, are produced in prolific quantities. They have the most wonderful colouring, with violet-blue central petals bordered by deep reddish-purple wings.

Sweet peas use tendrils to pull themselves up any handy support or through neighbouring plants and are often grown on a trellis, over an arch or up a timber or bamboo tripod, adding valuable height to the border. These hardy annuals are synonymous with scent and 'Matucana' doesn't disappoint. Its fragrance is intense and pervades the air around the flowers. Among the most endearing of all plants, sweet peas bring cottage garden appeal to the most suburban plot, flower endlessly through the summer and perfume the garden. Regular picking will sustain flowering for as long as possible and it's lovely to bring some of the fragrance into the house.

Lathyrus odoratus 'Matucana'
COMMON NAME Sweet pea
HARDINESS Fully hardy
ZONE 6
HEIGHT 2m (6½ft)
CULTIVATION Fertile, humus-rich, well-drained soil. Full sun to partial shade.
OTHER VARIETIES *Lathyrus odoratus* 'Charlie's Angel' – true blue flowers with excellent scent. *L. odoratus* 'Painted Lady' – sweet fragrance, deep pink and white flowers. *L. odoratus* 'Wedding Day' – pure white flowers and a lovely scent.

Rhodochiton atrosanguineus

My first encounter with this elegant climber was in the magnificent kitchen garden at the Old Rectory, Farnborough, where tall supports smothered with its pendulous flowers are placed strategically among the vegetables. Annual climbers are fast growing and give a real boost to dull trellis and empty walls or fences. A perennial in its native Mexico, in this country it is generally treated as an annual, although it may survive the winter in warm, sheltered areas. Plant out young seedlings when there is no danger of frost and they will quickly reach skyward using twining stalks.

The heart-shaped leaves are reminiscent of ivy, with a thinner, more matt texture and a deep red tinge to their edges. The pendulous flowers bring a touch of exoticism to the garden. Their outer petals form a bell shape like a magenta-pink pixie cap, inside which hangs a tubula flower of burgundy so deep it is almost black. The abundant flowers are suspended on thread-like stalks from the long stems and cover the entire plant. They are at their best in late summer and early autumn and are all the more welcome at a time when much of the garden has passed its best.

Rhodochiton atrosanguineus
COMMON NAME Purple bell vine
HARDINESS Frost tender
ZONE 9
HEIGHT 3m (10ft)
CULTIVATION Fertile, humus-rich, moist but well-drained soil. Full sun.

Nigella damascena 'Miss Jekyll' I never tire of this old favourite, which is blessed with perfection in both foliage and flower. Its common name, love-in-a-mist, perfectly describes the appeal of an airy plant studded with pretty flowers. The hazy effect it creates is produced by a bright green web of finely dissected, feathery foliage. A lacy collar of needle-fine leaves also surrounds each powder-blue, semi-double flower. These are produced in abundance throughout the summer, at the end of which the petals fall to reveal gooseberry-shaped seed-pods. These are extremely decorative and are often used for cutting and drying; remove the remaining stems at the end of the summer and hang them upside down in a warm, dry place. Alternatively, leave them in place to allow the plant to self-seed.

As a hardy annual, nigella can be sown in late summer or early autumn directly where it is to flower the following year – in fact it positively dislikes being transplanted. Simply thin the seedlings when they appear. It is an excellent mixer plant, blurring hard edges and blending with neighbouring plants in an unobtrusive way that is nonetheless key to the success of the overall combination. Sow the seeds in generous drifts to soften perennials with spiky or rounded leaves and weave them randomly through other hardy annuals.

Nigella damascena 'Miss Jekyll'
COMMON NAME Love-in-a-mist
HARDINESS Fully hardy
ZONE 6
HEIGHT 45–60cm (18–24in)
SPREAD 20cm (8in)
CULTIVATION Fertile, well-drained soil. Full sun.

Smyrnium perfoliatum This underused biennial first came to my attention at the Chelsea Physic Garden in London where it grows in a swathe beneath deciduous trees and shrubs. Christopher Lloyd also uses it to good effect in his garden, Great Dixter, in East Sussex, while at the Royal Horticultural Society Garden, Wisley, in Surrey, it is combined with late-flowering tulips. *Smyrnium perfoliatum* is easily confused with some of the similarly coloured euphorbias to which it bears a passing resemblance. The lower leaves are dark green, but they become smaller and brighter as they rise up the stems. The uppermost leaves appear to surround the slender stem completely, giving the impression that the stem is growing right through the middle of the leaf.

Small, flat clusters of vibrant, acidic yellow-green flowers are produced at the tips of the branching stems in late spring and early summer. This is one of my favourite colours in the garden; I use it to provide a striking contrast to strong shades such as regal purple, gentian blue, scarlet and magenta. These shocking colour combinations are not for the faint hearted, but they can be extremely effective. More subtle partnerships can be made with white-flowered plants, particularly those with a hint of green such as the Viridiflora tulip, *Tulipa* 'Spring Green'. Although it copes well with full sun, *Smyrnium perfoliatum* also grows very successfully in dappled shade where it can be allowed to self-seed and meander through shade-loving perennials in a woodland garden setting.

Smyrnium perfoliatum

COMMON NAME Perfoliate deseanders
HARDINESS Fully hardy
ZONE 6
HEIGHT 0.5–1.5m (2–5ft)
SPREAD 45cm (18in)
CULTIVATION Fertile, humus-rich, moist but well-drained soil. Full sun.

Eschscholzia californica

Eschscholzia californica There are few sights as cheerful in the mid-summer garden as a carpet of gold and orange California poppies. These natives of western North America and the State flower of California bear a profusion of single flowers in shades of deep yellow and tangerine. Although small at about 7cm (2¾in) across, the cup-shaped flowers are plentiful and complemented by delicate, lacy foliage with a slightly bluish tinge. There are various strains available, covering a colour spectrum that ranges from scarlet and pink to lemon and white, as well as ruffled double blooms, but my preference is for the unadulterated simplicity of the original.

An easy-to-grow hardy annual, the seeds are best sown thinly where they are to grow because the young seedlings dislike disturbance. Sow either in autumn to flower the following summer or in mid-spring to flower the same year. For best results choose a hot, sunny spot with well-drained soil where they will happily self-seed; growing them through gravel is particularly effective. Reaching about 35cm (14in) tall, they make a vibrant foreground for taller plants. Deadhead regularly to keep the flowers coming and don't forget to sow enough to allow you to pick a few for the house. This is best done when they are still tightly furled because the blooms, although lovely, last fleetingly once cut.

Eschscholzia californica

COMMON NAME California poppy
HARDINESS Fully hardy
ZONE 9
HEIGHT 35cm (14in)
SPREAD 15cm (6in)
CULTIVATION Moderately fertile, well-drained soil. Full sun.

Tithonia rotundifolia 'Torch'

There's no doubting the desirability of subtle plants in soft pastel shades, but sometimes what's needed is an injection of the wow factor. *Tithonia rotundifolia* 'Torch' delivers plenty of impact. It is a half-hardy annual, which means that it cannot overwinter successfully in our wet climate and needs to be sown under cover in early spring, ready to plant out after the frosts are over. Your efforts will be amply rewarded with strongly growing plants with attractive, grey-green foliage and an abundance of slender flowering stems from late summer into autumn.

The eye-catching flowers have daisy-like, deep orange, velvety petals encircling a ring of dark golden stamens, a richly saturated colour combination that gives the flowers a rare intensity and substance. The tall stems add valuable height to the border, where they can be grown right at the back, but they will need staking to prevent wind damage. In the long, hot-coloured border at Sutton Place in Surrey, a large clump of these knockout plants holds court over the lower-growing perennials, adding extra drama to an already lively scene. They look gorgeous with scarlet, tangerine and acid green companion plants – particularly those with bronze foliage – and are also invaluable as cut flowers.

Tithonia rotundifolia 'Torch'

COMMON NAME
  Mexican sunflower
HARDINESS Half hardy
ZONE 10
HEIGHT 1.5m (5ft)
SPREAD 30cm (1ft)
CULTIVATION Moderately
  fertile, well-drained soil.
  Full sun.

grasses

This group of plants has enjoyed an enormous surge in popularity in recent years. Not long ago, the only grass in the garden was the lawn and it would have been unthinkable to fill the herbaceous border with such 'wild' plants. It may have something to do with the fashion for loosening up planting schemes and an increasingly naturalistic style in garden design, but grasses are now integral to the contemporary garden and have infiltrated even the most traditional English country gardens. They have become much more than a temporary fad; now that we have discovered how beautiful and valuable grasses can be as garden plants, we will not let them go.

Grasses are surprisingly easy to place: they look at home with the most unlikely companions and their contribution adds greatly to the effectiveness of planting schemes. I prefer to mix grasses in the border with other perennials, annuals and shrubs, rather than confine them to a specific area. However, grasses are not reliant on the company of other plants; they are perfectly capable of shining on their own. Many are particularly well suited to growing as a single specimen plant that dominates one area of the garden. Others work beautifully in containers, adding grace to minimalist, modern garden designs.

Perhaps their most prized characteristic is the elegance of their form. Their arching stems, airy flowers and the liquid shapes they create while swaying in the wind give them a unique quality that has become essential to the overall success of planting combinations. There is endless variety in height, shape and habit, with something to suit every situation. Grasses range from neat, low-growing, spiky tufts, to tall, arching stems of airy grandeur. Some rely on breathtaking flowers or seed-heads to gain our attention, while others simply have beautiful foliage.

The whole spectrum of leaf colour is represented among the dazzling array of grasses available to the gardener. On offer is every shade of green from palest to darkest, plus glaucous blue-grey, acidic yellow-green, bronze, dark purple and deep red. Foliage may be needle-fine or ribbon-like, rough or smooth, variegated or plain. Flowers are the icing on the cake: delicate shimmering panicles of tiny seeds, squirrel tails as soft as spun silk, or frothy, gossamer-like inflorescences. The one thing they have in common is that no one can resist touching them.

Grasses are generally low-maintenance plants. Evergreen perennial grasses need little more than a quick tidy up in spring to remove dead leaves. Deciduous perennial grasses can be cut to the base in autumn if you like a neat garden, or left in situ over the winter where they continue to add structure and interest through the cold months, sparkling with early morning frost. Annuals are an oft-neglected group that are also hassle-free; many can simply be seeded where they are to flower later in the year. Whichever type you choose, if you are new to grasses, prepare to lose your heart.

Hakonechloa macra 'Aureola' This grass

has all the attributes of a highly desirable plant; in fact, I cannot think of a single thing to fault it. It forms a compact mound of rich yellow leaves streaked with green – colours that merge from a distance into vivid chartreuse. The rounded clumps of foliage are not only beautiful, but also non-invasive, making it easy to place in the garden or grow in a container. The individual blades of grass have a slender, bamboo-like appearance, giving the plant an exotic quality that is perfect for Japanese-style gardens or modern, minimalist settings. Perhaps its biggest boon is shade tolerance; grasses that will thrive at the front of a shady border are like gold dust and the luminous quality of the foliage adds to its value in the darker corners of the garden.

Be patient with the small plant you buy from the garden centre; it may not be fast growing, but it will eventually fill out into an impressive specimen. In my garden, it thrives on the front edge of a border in semi-shade. Making a reliable appearance each spring, it continues to look good throughout the summer and well into autumn when it takes on a more golden hue. Now in its fifth year, it forms an arching wave of brightly coloured leaves whose tips just touch the edge of the lawn. As well as brightening an area of mid-green and purple foliage, it adds a touch of class to the whole garden.

Hakonechloa macra 'Aureola'

COMMON NAME Hakone grass
HARDINESS Fully hardy
ZONE 5
HEIGHT 35cm (14in)
SPREAD 40cm (16in)
CULTIVATION Fertile, humus-rich, moist but well-drained soil. Sun to partial shade.

Pennisetum alopecuroides 'Hameln'

I recently designed a planting scheme for a show garden at *BBC Gardeners' World Live* in Birmingham using a lively combination of plants. The result was even better than I had hoped for, with the garden gaining plenty of attention from visitors, and the plant that attracted the most comments – all of them favourable – was *Pennisetum alopecuroides* 'Hameln'.

All the pennisetums are highly desirable grasses: they have an elegant shape, graceful, arching stems and tactile, furry flowers. Unfortunately, they will only give their best in a warm, sunny situation and getting them to flower in this country before temperatures begin to drop is always a bit of a gamble. I am happy to take the chance when the rewards are so great, but I would only recommend this grass if you can provide a really sheltered spot in full sun.

When it does flower well, the results are outstanding: a compact clump of slender, green foliage surmounted by dozens of thin stems carrying fluffy, bottle-brush flowers. These slender, creamy coloured, squirrel tails become pinky bronze towards autumn. They undoubtedly look lovely, but above all they are wonderful to touch, with an irresistibly strokeable quality. Grow them in a large swathe for maximum impact or put one in a pot on a sunny patio and wait for the compliments.

Pennisetum alopecuroides 'Hameln'

COMMON NAME Fountain grass

HARDINESS Fully hardy

ZONE 6

HEIGHT 45cm (18in)

SPREAD 60cm (2ft)

CULTIVATION Light, moderately fertile, well-drained soil. Full sun.

OTHER VARIETIES
Pennisetum orientale – fresh green foliage and pink-tinged flowers.
P. setaceum 'Rubrum' – deep burgundy foliage and wine red plumes of flowers. Not hardy, but will flower all year if overwintered in a warm, bright place.
P. villosum – pretty grass with pale green leaves and fluffy, creamy white flowers.

Elymus hispidus

Of all the perennial grasses in the blue-grey spectrum, this has arguably the most intense colouring. The shade is strongest early in the season, paling to creamy silver by the end of the autumn. Glaucous foliage is a real asset in the garden, cooling the tone of the surrounding planting and combining well with white and a wide range of flower colours. The pale silver-blue leaves provide an excellent contrast with neighbouring plants and their narrow shape works beautifully as a foil to broader leaves; blue-toned hostas make perfect partners. This is a grass to grow for its foliage; the flowers, which appear on slender stems in early summer, are secondary to the leaves.

There are several low-growing, tufted, blue-leaved grasses, but this one achieves a bit more height than most and can hold its own within a mixed or herbaceous border. Its vertical stems gently arch towards the top, giving a slightly unkempt appearance that helps to loosen a static group of plants and brings an attractive disorder to the scene. This is an excellent grass for a modern planting scheme; it suits the sleek metal, glass and perspex of minimalist gardens and looks perfectly at home grown through gravel with succulents, such as sedums and sempervivums, for company.

Elymus hispidus
COMMON NAME Blue wheatgrass
HARDINESS Fully hardy
ZONE 5
HEIGHT 75cm (30in)
SPREAD 40cm (16in)
CULTIVATION Moderately fertile, moist but well-drained soil. Full sun.

Miscanthus sinensis 'Zebrinus'

This deciduous perennial grass is always distinctive. Its gently arching, mid-green leaves are banded with horizontal stripes of creamy yellow, as if they have been tie-dyed. Upright stems produce spiky plumes of silken flowers in late summer, which are pinky bronze at first, becoming silvered towards autumn. With the double impact of attractive foliage and flowers, this grass represents excellent value in the garden. It is sometimes confused with the similar, but rather more erect *M. sinensis* 'Strictus' and is the slightly more hardy of the two, making it a good choice for an exposed garden.

All forms of *M. sinensis* work well in a sunny, mixed or herbaceous border, either as single specimens or planted in a large swathe. The vertical stems and leaves provide height and structure and contrast beautifully with rounded or broad-shaped neighbouring plants. The movement of both foliage and flowers in the wind will soften an otherwise static planting scheme, and the vivid variegation enlivens the whole scene. Don't be tempted to cut down the dying stems during the autumn tidy up. Leave the dead flower-heads in place through the winter to give vertical structure to the border and sparkle in the frost. Cut all the stems right down to the base in early spring before the new growth appears.

Miscanthus sinensis 'Zebrinus'

COMMON NAME Zebra grass
HARDINESS Fully hardy
ZONE 6
HEIGHT 1.5m (5ft)
SPREAD 1.2m (4ft)
CULTIVATION Fertile, humus-rich, moist soil. Full sun to partial shade.
OTHER VARIETIES
Miscanthus sinensis 'Silberfeder' – light purple, feathered flowers that turn to pale silver as they age.
M. sinensis 'Variegatus' – the striking, green and white variegated, arching foliage needs plenty of space to look its best.
M. sinensis 'Yakushima Dwarf' – compact form with pinky brown flowers, only 1m (3⅓ft) tall.

Lagurus ovatus
Grasses attract plenty of attention at the major flower shows and *Lagurus ovatus* always walks off the stands, despite the fact that it is a hardy annual. There are many lovely annual grasses and this is one of the best. Its tufts of slender, pale green leaves are pretty enough, but the real highlights are the flower-heads. Lovely, light green, fluffy flowers appear in abundance, atop needle-fine stems throughout the summer, each one like the softest make-up brush. If you want to dry the flowers, pick them while they are still young; otherwise, leave them to mature to pale buff-cream.

I like to place this grass where the low summer sun will backlight the flame-shaped flower-heads. It looks particularly pretty drifting informally through other sun-loving annuals or softening the permanent planting of perennials, but grows equally well in containers. Seed can be sown in situ in late summer to flower the following year, or in spring to flower the same year. You can also sow in pots during the spring. Alternatively, buy young plants from specialist nurseries when they become available in early summer. This is one of the most enchanting of all grasses; it doesn't take up much space and is irresistible to adults and children alike.

Lagurus ovatus
COMMON NAME Hare's tail
HARDINESS Fully hardy
ZONE 9
HEIGHT 50cm (20in)
SPREAD 30cm (12in)
CULTIVATION Moderately fertile, light, well-drained soil. Full sun.

Imperata cylindrica 'Rubra' I cannot praise this perennial grass too highly, and have watched its increasing popularity with pleasure. It has an elegant and well-behaved growth habit, with slow-spreading clumps of slender, upright leaves. Early in the season the leaves are bright green with vivid, blood-red tips. As the summer progresses the red becomes increasingly intense, so that by autumn most of the leaf is glowing crimson. I always try to position this grass where it will be back-lit by the late afternoon sun – raising it by planting in a container can help. The light makes the foliage glow like a beacon; a stunning effect.

The leaves provide a vertical accent that is a perfect foil for plants of a similar height with contrasting foliage and flowers. Place the imperata plants about 30cm (1ft) apart and intersperse them with flowering perennials to create a random effect. I have combined them most successfully with the chocolate cosmos, *Cosmos atrosanguineus* (page 86), whose deep burgundy flowers and stems pick up the red in the leaves of the grass, adding a generous helping of dazzling orange *Eschscholzia californica* (page 122) for contrast. Alternatively, place a large group of imperata together to fill a well-defined area with a carpet of intensely coloured foliage.

Imperata cylindrica 'Rubra'
COMMON NAME Japanese blood grass
HARDINESS Frost hardy
ZONE 7
HEIGHT 40cm (16in)
SPREAD 30cm (12in)
CULTIVATION Fertile, humus-rich, moist soil. Full sun to partial shade.

Stipa arundinacea I bought my first grass when the vogue for using them as mainstream garden plants was still in its infancy. It was a *Stipa arundinacea* and it remains one of my favourites to this day. It is a constant factor in my garden, looking good year in year out, and grows happily in a spot that only gets sun for half the day. I love this grass, not only for its easy-going nature, but for the compactness of its arching mound of attractive, evergreen foliage, and also its colour – the leaves are a dark yellowish-green early in the season, turning to shades of bronze and orange in autumn.

Panicles of tiny flowers are almost incidental to its beauty, but they do add an airy lightness to the clump of foliage from mid-summer onwards. Grow this grass as a single specimen or dotted throughout the border, where it associates well with summer-flowering bulbs, such as alliums, and subtle mauve and aubergine-coloured perennials. Alternatively, liven things up by giving it the orange *Canna* Tropicanna or *Dahlia* 'David Howard' for company. Established plants need a quick tidy up in early spring to remove any dead leaves. Self-seeded young plants will settle into any promising nooks and crannies and look after themselves.

Stipa arundinacea
COMMON NAME
  Pheasant's tail grass
HARDINESS Frost hardy
ZONE 8
HEIGHT 1m (3ft)
SPREAD 1.2m (4ft)
CULTIVATION Moderately
  fertile, well-drained soil.
  Full sun or partial shade.

Stipa tenuissima This is a wonderfully tactile grass: its flowers have the gossamer texture of spun silk and it is hard to resist brushing a hand through the downy flowers. A deciduous perennial, the plant consists of vertical tufts of very slender leaves, which are bulked up considerably throughout the summer by the cloud-like flowers.

There are many uses for *Stipa tenuissima*, but because it moves so beautifully in the gentlest breeze it is particularly effective grown in swathes or long rows, where it takes on the wave-like appearance of rippling water, ebbing and flowing in the wind. It is also a perfect blending plant, blurring the hard edges of more structured neighbours. Planted in front of taller perennials, its softening effect will instantly bring a traditional herbaceous border bang up to date, and groups of three or more positioned close to the side of a raised bed, or in a container, will billow gently over the edge.

Whenever it starts to look messy – anytime between late autumn and early spring – cut back the old stems to make way for new growth. This is not a long-lived grass so expect to replant from time to time, unless, of course, you're happy to allow the self-sown seedlings to choose their own spot. Either way, no garden should be without it; for me the airy movement and touchy-feely qualities make this a must-have plant.

Stipa tenuissima
COMMON NAME Feather grass
HARDINESS Fully hardy
ZONE 7
HEIGHT 60cm (2ft)
SPREAD 30cm (12in)
CULTIVATION Moderately fertile, well-drained soil. Full sun.

winter-flowering shrubs

It's easy to be seduced by the ample charms of the summer garden, but the subtle delights to be found in winter should not be overlooked. Many of the best public and botanic gardens feature a winter garden or border – some very extensive – that is filled entirely with plants that come into their own in mid-winter. Others are sure to include winter-interest planting among their schemes, achieving a balance that attracts the off-season visitor. Large, private gardens may have the luxury of space to do the same and are increasingly beginning to do so. The time has also come for the small, private garden to refuse to roll over and go to sleep during the winter months.

For over a third of each year, from late October to late March, our gardens can be dreary places. If the bulk of the planting is geared around spring and summer, with perhaps a nod toward autumn, there will be no room to accommodate the wealth of plants that peak in the fourth season. A single visit to a garden with a winter border will show sceptical gardeners what they are missing by ignoring these plant. The sheer beauty and variety can be surprising, taking inspiration from these gardens will prevent their plot from going into annual hibernation.

Winter interest can be found in the colour and texture of stems and bark, the glow of scarlet and orange berries and a wealth of decorative, evergreen foliage. These plants rightly form the backbone of the year-round garden, but it's easy to forget that some of the loveliest of all flowers also appear at this time of year. They tend on the whole to be small, but make up for this by being grouped together in clusters. Colours are often particularly fresh and pretty, with sugar pink and yellow featuring strongly.

As a bonus, nature gives many of these exquisite but diminutive flowers the most intense and delicious perfume. The scent of even the smallest flower can be really powerful and hit you unexpectedly from the other side of the garden. On sunny days the fragrance carries on the warmed air, bringing with it the promise of spring. Position your winter performers where you will get the full impact of their fragrance or plant them a bit further away as an irresistible incentive to venture outside on a cold, bright day.

If you cannot be tempted outdoors, an attractive view from the window will still give pleasure. This is the time of year to sit and contemplate the garden and decide how it might be improved for the coming year. When you make your plans, ask yourself whether it is providing year-round enjoyment. Every garden should have at least one shrub for winter interest and once you have discovered the wealth of beauty to be found at this time of year you will be prepared to sacrifice a bit of summer colour for a more balanced garden.

Skimmia × confusa 'Kew Green' It may be tempting to fill your garden with exotic, rare or unusual plants, but every well-designed planting scheme needs a high proportion of good doers to form the backbone of the planting and tie all the exotic lovelies together. Skimmias are incredibly useful, fool-proof shrubs that can cope with sun or shade and require no pruning. Their low growth habit and compact shape fill a gap and provide[[a year-round backdrop of evergreen foliage. They are available in male, female or hermaphrodite forms, which means that they produce either flowers or berries or a combination of the two. *Skimmia × confusa* 'Kew Green' is a male form with glossy, mid-green leaves and cone-shaped clusters of tiny, rounded buds that open in early spring to reveal creamy white flowers with a hint of green.

This is a shrub with a simplicity of style and neatness of habit that gives it enormous appeal; it walks off the shelves at garden centres. Give it a bit of acidity in the soil and neither very dry nor very wet conditions and you will have an attractive addition to the border. Rather than planting just a single specimen, try grouping several plants together – a technique employed with great success in the inspirational winter borders at Capel Manor in Middlesex – or put one in a large container and surround it with winter-flowering cyclamen and dwarf narcissi.

Skimmia × confusa
'Kew Green'
HARDINESS Fully hardy
ZONE 6
HEIGHT 0.5–3m (1.5–10ft)
SPREAD 1.5m (5ft)
CULTIVATION Fertile, humus-rich, moist but well-drained, neutral to slightly acid soil. Sun to partial shade.

Viburnum × bodnantense 'Dawn'

This excelllent shrub is guaranteed to make you relish a bright, cold, winter day. During summer it is clothed in dark green serrated leaves, which provide a useful backdrop for the showy flowers of surrounding plants. However, as winter begins to take hold, it comes into its own. Clusters of intensely scented flowers appear on the bare stems, each tiny, trumpet-shaped bloom opening a deep, rosy pink and fading gradually to palest shell pink, an effect that reminds me of raspberry ripple ice-cream. Flowering lasts for several months despite the inevitable inclement weather; the tiny blooms can withstand frost, although damage may occur when strong morning sunshine falls on recently frosted petals. Happily, new flowers soon take their place.

When several plants are grouped together, the effect is particularly striking. They are tall enough to provide screening from neighbouring gardens and can be grown as an informal boundary, dividing one section of a large garden from another. This is a tough, easy-to-grow shrub that requires neither cosseting or pruning. If you have room for only a single winter-interest shrub, the contribution made by its pretty, long-lasting, honey-scented flowers should put this viburnum firmly at the top of your list.

Viburnum × *bodnantense* 'Dawn'
HARDINESS Fully hardy
ZONE 5
HEIGHT 3m (10ft)
SPREAD 2m (6½ft)
CULTIVATION Moderately fertile, moist but well-drained soil. Full sun to partial shade.
OTHER VARIETIES *Viburnum tinus* 'Eve Price' – this familiar favourite is the staple of many gardens. Its evergreen foliage, bushy habit and clusters of white flowers that open from pink buds in late winter and early spring justify its popularity. *V. farreri* – a deciduous shrub with strongly perfumed, creamy white flowers flushed with pink, followed by good autumn tints and scarlet berries. *V. farreri* 'Candidissimum' – white-flowered form of the species, with pale yellow berries.

Sarcococca hookeriana var. digyna 'Purple Stem'

The Christmas box is one of the shrubs that I recommend most frequently for difficult, shady sites. It may not be the showiest specimen, but it has many lovely features, and although it is undoubtedly a useful plant, it is highly desirable in its own right. Among its attributes are slender, evergreen leaves, whose young stems are tinged wine red. Winter brings tiny, fringed, creamy white flowers hidden in the leaf axels. They are not much to look at, yet produce an intense, vanilla scent, the impact of which is disproportionate to their size. The flowers are followed by shiny, black berries, which nestle among the foliage.

This shrub is hard to beat for large-scale underplanting of deciduous trees and tall shrubs or for providing tall, evergreen ground cover. If you have sufficient space I suggest planting it in a group of three or more for maximum impact, but even a single plant is a welcome addition to the smaller garden. With a compact growth habit, the ability to thrive in full shade or a more open position, a tolerance of any type or quality of soil and minimal, if any, pruning requirements, you will not regret including one in your planting scheme. Sarcococcas are generally an under-used group of shrubs and in my opinion every shady garden should have at least one.

Sarcococca hookeriana var. *digyna* 'Purple Stem'
COMMON NAME Christmas box
HARDINESS Fully hardy
ZONE 5
HEIGHT 1.5m (5ft)
SPREAD 2m (6½ft)
CULTIVATION Moderately fertile, humus-rich, moist but
 well-drained soil. Sun to full shade.

Chimonanthus praecox 'Grandiflorus' This large shrub could never be described as a show-stopper in the summer and its lack of year-round interest makes it unsuitable for small gardens, but in winter it more than redeems itself to earn a place in a sizeable plot. Wintersweet may take several years to become established and start flowering, but the results are worth waiting for, with ample compensation in the form of deliciously scented flowers. These appear in late winter when the garden is at its bleakest and least promising, clinging closely to the bare, twiggy stems. Their creamy yellow petals have a waxy texture, the bases of each one stained with a characteristic, deep maroon blotch.

The chief glory of this otherwise subtle plant is its scent, an intensely sweet and fruity fragrance that is carried across the garden on the warm air of a clear, winter day. A sheltered, sunny spot will encourage flowering and, therefore, the strongest perfume. I have seen it grown very successfully as a wall shrub, trained and tied in to supports on a house wall. Grow a clematis through the branches to add interest to the large, willow-like foliage in summer. Chimonanthus will thrive on fertile soil that is regularly improved with generous amounts of bulky organic matter; treat it well and you will be rewarded with an unusual shrub whose subtle yet distinctive charms far outweigh its shortcomings.

Chimonanthus praecox 'Grandiflorus'
COMMON NAME Wintersweet
HARDINESS Fully hardy
ZONE 7
HEIGHT 4m (12ft)
SPREAD 3m (10ft)
CULTIVATION Fertile, moist but well-drained soil. Full sun.

Hamamelis × intermedia 'Pallida'

My favourite witch hazel is a hybrid of the Japanese *Hamamelis japonica* and the Chinese *Hamamelis mollis*. It eventually grows in stature to become something between a large shrub and a small tree with a vase-shaped form. A profusion of strange, spidery flowers with good fragrance appear in clusters on the bare stems in late winter. They are a clear, bright, lemon yellow – a fresh, sulphurous colour that makes the entire shrub highly visible and very striking from a distance. Although unremarkable through the summer, the foliage provides good autumn tints of brilliant orange and gold.

All witch hazels need a bit of initial coaxing to do well. They will thrive in a sheltered position with a reasonably acidic soil and hate to be disturbed once they are established. They look extremely effective when grown in groups of three or more in a large woodland garden or a border planted for winter interest. If space is limited, select a single specimen and underplant it with bulbs and perennials. When in flower, this plant lights up the winter garden like a beacon. There is no doubt that witch hazels are rather alien-looking plants, but that is part of their appeal – there is nothing else quite like them.

Hamamelis × intermedia 'Pallida'
COMMON NAME Witch hazel
HARDINESS Fully hardy
ZONE 5
HEIGHT 4m (13ft)
SPREAD 4m (13ft)
CULTIVATION Moderately fertile, moist but well-drained, neutral to acid soil. Full sun to partial shade.

Daphne odora 'Aureomarginata' There is much to recommend this lovely shrub. Its attractive, compact growth makes it ideal for the smaller garden, while its glossy, evergreen leaves edged with a narrow margin of pale gold are good to look at all year round. The straightforward *Daphne odora* is equally useful, but lacks the variegation. Having spent much of January in bud, the flowers open in my London garden in early February. Clusters of small, pure white trumpets nestle among the leaves, the backs of each petal flushed a deep, rosy pink, making a refreshingly pretty combination. Emanating from these innocent-looking flowers is an intoxicating, honeyed fragrance that is well worth venturing outside for on a cold day.

Daphnes have a reputation for being temperamental, but I find this one generally undemanding. The trick is to prevent the soil from drying out completely in summer or getting waterlogged in winter: if you can achieve this balance you should have no problems. A lightly shaded spot is ideal, where they make perfect fillers among larger, deciduous shrubs and trees. This shrub has a pleasing natural form that does not require shaping; pruning should be avoided in any case because it may cause part of the shrub to die back. This is a classy plant with low-maintenance requirements, good garden value and among the very best perfume. It gives non-stop pleasure throughout the year.

Daphne odora 'Aureomarginata'

HARDINESS Frost hardy to fully hardy

ZONE 7

HEIGHT 1.5m (5ft)

SPREAD 1.5m (5ft)

CULTIVATION Moderately fertile, humus-rich, moist but well-drained soil. Sun to partial shade.

OTHER VARIETIES *Daphne bholua* 'Jacqueline Postill' – highly scented, sugar-pink flowers from mid-winter to early spring. *D. mezereum* – bare winter stems studded with rich purple flowers.

index

ACKNOWLEDGEMENTS

I am indebted to the following at BBC Worldwide for their patience and guidance: Robin Wood, Viv Bowler, Helena Caldon and Julie-Anne Hutchinson. Grateful thanks also to Isobel Gillan for her impeccable eye.

At the BBC I would like to thank Jane Root and Nicola Moody for their support and encouragement.

My thanks are also due to Tony Laryea, Colette Foster, Louise Hampden and all at Catalyst Television.

For their unfailing help and excellent advice my thanks to Annie Sweetbaum, Hilary Murray-Watts and all at Arlington Enterprises, and to Luigi Bonomi at Sheil Land Associates.

My thanks also to Ingrid Henningsson for her invaluable assistance and meticulous attention to detail, and to Harriet Fear Davis for painstakingly checking the proofs.

Without the constant support of my family this book would never have materialised. Heartfelt thanks to my parents Ghita and Michael Cohen, and my brothers Joshua, Daniel and Simon.

Above all, my love and gratitude to Gerard, Lauren and Joseph for continuing to inspire everything I do.

ADDITIONAL PICTURE CAPTIONS

page 1 *Rosa* 'Königin von Dänemark', 2 *Tulipa* 'Queen of Night', 4 *Miscanthus sinensis* 'Zebrinus', 6 and 7 *Iris pallida* subsp. *pallida*, 10 *Anthemis tinctoria* 'Sauce Hollandaise', 22 *Liquidamber styraciflua*, 34 *Rodgersia*, 48 *Stipa gigantea*, 60 *Rosa* Gertrude Jekyll, 70 Silver birch bark, 80 *Papaver somniferum*, 94 *Clematis* Lasurstern, 104 *Foeniculum vulgare* 'Purpureum', 114 *Nigella damascena* 'Miss Jekyll' and *Eschscholzia californica*, 124 *Stipa tenuissima*, p134 *Hamamelis* x *intermedia* 'Pallida'.

CLIMATE ZONES

The zone ratings given for each plant in the index suggest the minimum and maximum temperatures a plant will tolerate. However, this can only be a rough guide as hardiness depends on a great many factors.

Celsius	Zones	Fahrenheit
Below −45	1	below −50
−45 to −40	2	−50 to −40
−40 to −34	3	−40 to −30
−34 to −29	4	−30 to −20
−29 to −23	5	−20 to −10
−23 to −18	6	−10 to 0
−18 to −12	7	0 to 10
−12 to −7	8	10 to 20
−7 to −1	9	20 to 30
−1 to −4	10	30 to 40
above 4	11	above 40

This book is published to accompany the television series *Gardeners' World*, produced for BBC2 by Catalyst Television Limited.

Series producer: Colette Foster
Executive producer: Tony Laryea

Published by BBC Worldwide Limited
Woodlands
80 Wood Lane
London W12 0TT

First published 2002
Copyright © Rachel de Thame 2002
The moral right of the author has been asserted.

Pictures copyright:
Jonathan Buckley, 4, 13,14, 22, 32, 39, 40–1, 45, 50, 57, 60, 62, 65, 66, 72, 82, 83, 87, 88, 93, 94, 103, 109, 110, 114, 116, 117, 118, 120, 121, 122, 123, 124, 126, 129. 132, 139; Garden picture library © Howard Rice 10, 28, 29, 113 © Neil Holmes 38, 112; © David England 90–1, © Jerry Pavia 84–5; © Didier Willery 20; Jerry Harpur, 48, 53, 69, 108, 111, 137; Marcus Harper, 18, 19, 30–1, 37, 46–7, 52, 70, 75, 78, 79, 98, 104, 127, 141; Andrew Lawson, 1, 6–7, 16, 21, 26, 33, 51, 56, 64, 68, 73, 77, 80, 86, 92, 97, 99, 100, 101, 107, 119, 130, 133, 140; Marianne Majerus, 2, 43, 54–5, 58, 76, 96, 102, 106; S & O Mathews, 24–5, 27, 44; Clive Nichols, 12, 15, 17, 34, 36, 42, 67, 74, 89, 131, 134, 136, 138; Photos horticultural, 63, 128; John Rogers/Staystill, 9.

ISBN: 0 563 53467 2

Commissioning editor: Vivien Bowler
Project editor: Helena Caldon
Copy-editor: Julie-Anne Hutchinson
Designer: Isobel Gillan
Production controller: Christopher Tinker

Set in Helvetica Neue
Printed and bound in Great Britain by Butler & Tanner Ltd, Frome
Colour separations by Radstock Reproductions Ltd, Midsomer Norton
Jacket printed by Lawrence-Allen Ltd, Weston-super-Mare